TANGO

DATE DUE

GAYLORD   PRINTED IN U.S.A.

TANGO

A play in three acts by

Slawomir Mrozek

Translated by
Ralph Manheim and Teresa Dzieduscycka

Grove Press, Inc., New York

Library of Congress Catalog Card Number: 67-27885

First Printing

Manufactured in the United States of America

Tango was first performed at the Jugoslovensko Dramsko Pozoriske in Belgrade, Yugoslavia on April 21, 1965. The first Polish performance took place in Warsaw on July 7, 1965 at the Teatr Wspołozesny, directed by Erwin Axer. The first performance of *Tango* in New York took place at the Pocket Theater on January 20, 1969. The production was staged by Heinz Engels and based on the original staging by Erwin Axer, with setting by Jason Phillips, costumes by John E. Hirsch, lighting by Paul Holland, and dance arranged by Jon Devlin. The cast was as follows:

EUGENIA	Muriel Kirkland
EDDIE	Clifford A. Pellow
EUGENE	Arthur Ed Forman
ARTHUR	David Margulies
ELEANOR	Lilyan Wilder
STOMIL	Stefan Schnabel
ALA	Elizabeth Swain

Photographs of the New York production by Arthur Cantor

TANGO

ACT ONE

A large, high room. The wall on the right ("right" and "left" are always taken from the point of view of the audience) is not visible. This gives the impression that the room extends beyond the edge of the stage. The wall on the left does not reach to the front of the stage but forms a right angle a few steps behind it and continues leftward along the proscenium. Between this corner of the wall and the left edge of the stage there is a door leading into a second room. This produces a kind of corridor leading offstage to the left and into the main room on the right. At the left and right of the rear wall, two more doors. The doors all look the same: double doors, high, painted a dark color, and ornamented in a style befitting old, solidly middle-class houses. Between the two doors in the rear wall, an alcove covered by a curtain. In the room: a table with eight chairs, armchairs, a couch, small tables, a large mirror on the left-hand wall. The furniture is arranged haphazardly as though the family had just moved in or were about to move out. Great confusion. In addition, the whole stage is full of draperies, hanging, lying or rolled, adding to the impression of confusion and blurring the outlines of the room. The room seems to be covered with spots. At one point on the floor draperies are thrown into a heap, forming a kind of bed. An old-fashioned black baby carriage on high, thin wheels. A dusty wedding dress. A derby hat. The velvet tablecloth is shoved half-aside. Three persons are seated at the uncovered part of the table. The first, who will be called

GRANDMA *for the present, is an elderly but well-preserved and lively lady, who suffers only occasionally from senile absentmindedness. Her dress, in a garish-colored flower pattern, has a train attached; she wears a jockey cap and sneakers. She seems to be near-sighted. A gray-haired, extremely polite old man. He is wearing glasses with thin gold rims, but his dress is disordered, and he seems dusty and intimidated. Swallow-tail coat, dirty stiff collar, a wide tie with a pearl stickpin, but khaki-colored shorts, scotch-plaid knee socks, torn patent-leather shoes, bare knees. The third individual, who gives the impression of being crude and shady, wears baggy, light-gray, rumpled pants and an ugly checked shirt, open at the chest. His shirtsleeves are rolled up. He habitually scratches his fat behind. Long greasy hair, which he frequently combs with a comb which he takes from his back pocket. Small, square mustache. Unshaven. A watch with a shiny gold wristband. All three are deep in their card game. On the velvet tablecloth: dishes, cups, carafes, artificial flowers, scraps of food. But also a few incongruous objects: a large, empty, bottomless bird cage; a lady's shoe; a pair of riding breeches. Even more than the rest of the furnishings, this table gives an impression of haphazardness, eccentricity and disorder. Each plate comes from a different set, each object is of a different period and style. From the right enters a young man of twenty-five at the most: imposing and pleasant appearance. Neat, freshly pressed, ready-made suit that fits him perfectly, white shirt, tie. Under his arm he is carrying books and papers. He stands still and observes the scene. The three card players do not notice him. The table is quite far to the left. The person temporarily known as* GRANDMA *is sitting with her back to the young man, her profile to the audience. The elderly gentleman is facing her. At the head of the table the third player, with his back to the audience. The young man who has just come in is to one side of him.*

PERSON TEMPORARILY KNOWN AS GRANDMA *(throwing a card on the table with exaggerated gusto)*: Three of spades. Razor blades.

PLAYER WITH MUSTACHE *(throwing down a card)*: Down on the table goes old Aunt Mabel. *(He drinks beer from a bottle standing beside his chair.)*

OLD GENTLEMAN *(timidly clearing his throat; speaks with a visible effort)*: Indeed, yes. I mean. . . . Well, plunk! *(He throws down a card.)*

PERSON TEMPORARILY KNOWN AS GRANDMA *(waits for a moment, then with disapproval)*: Plunk! Oh come on, Eugene! Plunk what?

OLD GENTLEMAN *or* EUGENE *(stuttering helplessly)*: Plunk . . . plunk. . . .

PLAYER WITH MUSTACHE: The old gentleman's not in form today.

He takes a swig from the bottle.

PERSON TEMPORARILY KNOWN AS GRANDMA: Eugene! If you're going to play with us, you've got to do it right. Plunk's all right, but then what?

EUGENE: Well, just plain plunk!

PERSON TEMPORARILY KNOWN AS GRANDMA: Good Lord, you're blushing again!

EUGENE: Well then, plunk—trunk. Will that do?

PERSON TEMPORARILY KNOWN AS GRANDMA: Certainly not. Why don't you help him out, Eddie?

PLAYER WITH MUSTACHE *or* EDDIE: ith plunk? That's a tough word to work with. How about: Scram, Sam. We're on the lam.

EUGENE: Splendid! Splendid. But if you'll excuse my asking, what does it mean? Who's on the lam?

EDDIE: It's what they say, that's all.

PERSON TEMPORARILY KNOWN AS GRANDMA: Eugene. Eddie knows best.

EUGENE (*throwing the same card on the table again*): Scram, Sam. We're on the lam.

PERSON TEMPORARILY KNOWN AS GRANDMA: See, with a little effort you can do it too.

EDDIE: The old gentleman is a bit bashful.

PERSON TEMPORARILY KNOWN AS GRANDMA: Thank you, Eddie dear. I don't know what we would do without you.

EDDIE: Don't mention it. (*He sees the* YOUNG MAN *and quickly hides the bottle under the table.*) I'd better be leaving.

PERSON TEMPORARILY KNOWN AS GRANDMA: What? Why? What's got into you? Right in the middle of our game?

YOUNG MAN: Good morning!

PERSON TEMPORARILY KNOWN AS GRANDMA (*turns around, annoyed*): Oh, it's you.

YOUNG MAN: Yes, me. What's going on here anyway?

PERSON TEMPORARILY KNOWN AS GRANDMA: What do you mean? We're just having our little game.

YOUNG MAN: I can see that. But with whom?

PERSON TEMPORARILY KNOWN AS GRANDMA: With whom? Don't you recognize your Uncle Eugene any more?

YOUNG MAN: I wasn't asking about Uncle Eugene. I'll settle with him later. Who is this individual? (*He indicates* EDDIE.)

EDDIE (*stands up*): I'll just be running along now: Madam, the pleasure was mine.

PERSON TEMPORARILY KNOWN AS GRANDMA: Edward! Stay!

YOUNG MAN: Out! Out!

EDDIE (*reproachfully to* GRANDMA): Dear lady, didn't I tell you we shouldn't have played today?

EUGENE (*pointing to* GRANDMA): It's her fault. Entirely her fault. I didn't even want to play.

YOUNG MAN (*stepping up to the table*): I said Out!

EDDIE: Easy, Aces. I'm going!

On his way out he comes close to the YOUNG MAN. *He takes one of the books from under his arm and opens it.*

YOUNG MAN (*rushing toward the table*): How often have I told you never to let this happen again?

He runs around the table in pursuit of GRANDMA, *who tries to evade him.*

PERSON TEMPORARILY KNOWN AS GRANDMA: No! No!

YOUNG MAN: Oh yes, oh yes! And right now too!

EDDIE (*leafing through the book*): Fabulous!

PERSON TEMPORARILY KNOWN AS GRANDMA: What do you want of me anyway?

YOUNG MAN (*running after her*): You know very well what I want.

EUGENE: Arthur, have you no pity for your own grandmother?

YOUNG MAN, *or* ARTHUR: Oh, so you're talking back again are you, Uncle?

EUGENE: Not at all. I simply wanted to say that even if Eugenia may have forgotten herself a bit . . .

ARTHUR: Then I'll just have to remind her. And you too, Uncle. Pity! How can you talk about pity? Do any of you have any pity for me? Does she ever try to understand me? Oh, but this time, Uncle, you're going to get what's coming to you. Why aren't you working? Why aren't you writing your memoirs?

EUGENE: I did write a bit this morning, but then they came barging into my room, and . . .

PERSON HITHERTO KNOWN AS GRANDMA, *or* EUGENIA: Eugene! Traitor!

EUGENE (*hysterically*): Why can't you all just leave me in peace?

ARTHUR: Oh, we will. But you've got to be punished too. (*He puts the bottomless bird cage over Eugene's head.*) Now sit there until I let you out.

EUGENIA: Serves him right.

ARTHUR: Don't think you're going to get off free. (*He pulls back the curtain over the alcove, revealing a catafalque covered with a discolored black cloth and surmounted by several candelabra.*) Hup! Up you go!

EDDIE (*looking through the book with increasing interest*): Terrific! (*He sits down off to one side.*)

EUGENIA: Again? I don't want to!

ARTHUR: Not another word!

EUGENIA *humbly approaches the catafalque,* EUGENE *attentively offers her his arm.*

Up you go.

EUGENIA (*icily*): Thank you, Judas!

EUGENE: Your cards were no good anyway.

EUGENIA: Fool!

ARTHUR: This ought to cure you of your disgusting frivolity. (*Tapping his pockets.*) Matches! Who's got a match?

EUGENIA (*lying down on the catafalque*): At least spare me the candles, Arthur.

ARTHUR: Quiet, or I'll think up something really grim.

EDDIE (*without taking his eyes off the book, produces a box of matches*): Here!

ARTHUR *takes the matches, lights the candles.* EUGENE *takes the artificial flowers from the table, places them beside* EUGENIA, *takes a few steps back to examine the effect, adjusts the flowers again.*

Great pictures! (*He giggles.*)

EUGENIA (*raising her head*): What's he looking at?

ARTHUR: Lie down!

EUGENE (*steps up to* EDDIE *and looks over his shoulder*): Handbook of Anatomy.

EUGENIA: Just what he needs!

EDDIE: Is Mr. Arthur studying medicine?

EUGENE: He's studying for three different degrees. One in philosophy.

EDDIE: Is there something like this for philosophy?

EUGENE: Don't be ridiculous! They don't illustrate philosophy.

EDDIE: Too bad. It might be good.

EUGENIA (*sitting up*): Let me see!

ARTHUR: Lie down!

EUGENIA: To think that you're the youngest one of us all! Why don't you enter a monastery?

ARTHUR: Why do you simply refuse to understand me, Grandmother?

EUGENE: Yes, I've been wondering about that myself. Why do you refuse to understand him, Eugenia?

ARTHUR: I just can't live in a world like this!

ELEANOR *enters from the door on the extreme left. She has definitely crossed the threshold of middle age. She is wearing slacks with suspenders in the style of the 1930's.*

ELEANOR: What kind of world? What *are* you people doing?

ARTHUR: Good morning, Mother.

ELEANOR: Mama! On the catafalque again?

EUGENIA: A good thing you've come, Eleanor. Now you can see for yourself how he treats me.

ARTHUR: How *I* treat *you?* She had to be disciplined.

EUGENIA: He's trying to educate me.

ARTHUR: She really goes too far.

ELEANOR: What did she do?

ARTHUR: She knows.

ELEANOR: But why the catafalque?

ARTHUR: To remind her of eternity. Let her lie there and look within.

ELEANOR (*seeing* EDDIE): Ah, Eddie.

EDDIE: Hi!

ARTHUR: You mean you know each other?

EUGENE (*to himself*): Here we go.

ELEANOR: Everybody knows Eddie. Why not?

ARTHUR: I'm going mad. I come home and what do I find? Laxity, chaos, shady characters, ambiguous relationships. And on top of all that, it turns out that even you . . . No! No! Why does all this have to happen? Where is it all going to end?

ELEANOR: Perhaps you'd like something to eat?

ARTHUR: Eat? No. All I want is to get the situation under control.

ELEANOR: Oh Lord. I sleep with Eddie from time to time. Don't I, Eddie?

EDDIE (*absently*): What? Oh yes. Of course. (*He unfolds some color plates inserted in the book.*) Look at that! And all in color!

ARTHUR: What's that? What did you say, Mother?

ELEANOR: I'll get you something to eat. I won't be long.

> *She goes out through the door right rear.* ARTHUR *sits down distraught.*

EUGENE (*to himself*): She did put that a bit bluntly. I must say. (*To* ARTHUR.) May I take this off now? (*Silence.*) Arthur? (*Silence.*) Arthur! (*Silence.*) Arthur, I say, may I take this thing off now?

ARTHUR: Take it off. (*To himself.*) Nothing matters now.

EUGENE (*taking the bird cage off his head*): Thank you! (*He sits down next to* ARTHUR.) What's wrong, Arthur?

EUGENIA: Christ, this thing is hard!

EUGENE: I can understand that this business about your mother must be rather upsetting. I can well understand that. I'm an old-timer. (*Pause.*) Eddie's not a bad sort. He has a good heart even if he doesn't look very bright. (*More softly.*) Between you and me, he's not quite all there. . . . (*Louder.*) But what can you expect, my dear boy? Life must be taken as it is . . . (*more softly*) . . . or must it? (*Louder.*) Now, now, Arthur. Chin up! Eddie has his good points, and after all, my goodness . . . we've got to face up to it: your mother isn't quite what she used to be. (*More softly.*) You should have seen her when she was young, before you were born, of course. Even before Stomil came along . . . (*Ponders, moves his chair closer to* ARTHUR; *very softly.*) What are you planning to do about Eddie anyway? Frankly, he's a thoroughly bad sort. His fingernails are always so dirty. A sleazy type, wouldn't you say? And I'm convinced that he cheats at cards. He smacks his lips when he eats and he goes around here as if he owned the place. I wouldn't even shake hands with him if I weren't afraid of offending Eugenia. You know what he did yesterday? I go to Eugenia and I say: "Look here, it's fine with me if Eddie doesn't brush his teeth, but if he has to borrow my toothbrush, I wish he'd brush his teeth with it instead of his shoes." And what does he say? "There's nothing wrong with my teeth. They're white. They're sharp. But sometimes my shoes get dirty." That's what he says and then throws me out. I wouldn't want to influence you one way or another, but if I were you, I'd get rid of him. How about throwing him down the stairs? Hm?

ARTHUR: Oh, that wouldn't really solve anything.

EUGENE: Or maybe a left hook right in the face?

ARTHUR: That, too, would leave the basic situation unchanged.

EUGENE: Just a small one right in the face? It couldn't do any harm. If it's all right with you, I'll tell him to get ready for one.

EUGENIA *has meanwhile sat up and is listening. As soon as* EUGENE *notices this, he moves away from* ARTHUR. *Louder.*

Eddie is simple, yes, simple and very decent. I have never in all my years met a simpler man.

EUGENIA: What's wrong with him?

EUGENE: I don't know. He just doesn't react anymore.

EUGENIA: What are you whispering in his ear?

EUGENE: Me? Nothing. I've just been telling him about the life of the bees.

ELEANOR (*brings in a tray with a cup and cookies*): Breakfast is ready, Arthur!

ARTHUR (*waking out of his thoughts; automatically*): Thank you, Mother.

He sits down at the table. ELEANOR *sets the tray down in front of him, roughly shoving other objects aside.* ARTHUR *stirs his coffee. The tray is tilted up. He pulls a woman's shoe out from under it and heaves it angrily into the corner.*

EDDIE: Could you let me have this until Tuesday?

ARTHUR: I'm afraid not. I've got an exam on Monday.

EDDIE: Too bad. Some terrific pictures in here.

ELEANOR: Mother, get down off that thing, will you? You look like a character out of Edgar Allen Poe.

EUGENIA: A who, out of what?

ELEANOR: Oh, just like somebody on a catafalque. It's all so terribly old-fashioned.

EUGENIA (*motioning toward* ARTHUR): But what will he say?

ELEANOR: He's eating now. He won't say anything.

EUGENIA: Arthur, may I get down?

ARTHUR: It's all the same to me. (*He drinks.*) This coffee's bitter.

ELEANOR: We're all out of sugar. Eugene ate it.

EUGENE: I beg your pardon. All I ate was the jam. It was Eddie who ate up the sugar.

EUGENIA *comes down from the catafalque.*

ELEANOR: And blow those candles out, will you? We've got to economize. (*Looking at the cards.*) Who's winning?

EUGENIA: Eddie.

EUGENE: There is something positively unnatural about Edward's good luck.

ELEANOR: Eddie, have you been cheating?

EDDIE: Me? Never.

ELEANOR: You haven't? But you promised you'd lose today, remember? I need the money for groceries.

EDDIE (*throwing up his arms*): I must be a born winner. Tough luck!

Enter STOMIL, *Arthur's father. In pajamas, sleepy. Yawning and scratching himself. He is a large, corpulent man with gray hair like a lion's mane.*

STOMIL: I smelled coffee. (*Catching sight of* EDDIE.) Hello, Eddie.

ARTHUR *thrusts the tray aside and observes the scene with tense interest.*

ELEANOR: I thought this was your day to sleep until noon. The bed will be occupied after lunch.

STOMIL: I can't sleep. A whole new idea suddenly came to me. Who's drinking coffee anyway? Oh, it's you, Arthur . . . (*He steps up to the table.*)

ARTHUR (*disgustedly*): Good God, Father, can't you at least button up your pajamas?

STOMIL: What for?

ARTHUR: What for? What do you mean, what for?

STOMIL: I mean: What for? Such a simple question and you can't find an answer.

ARTHUR: Because . . . because one just doesn't appear like that.

STOMIL (*drinking Arthur's coffee*): You see? Your answer is meaningless. It's pure convention. It won't stand up under the scrutiny of the intellect.

ARTHUR: Isn't that enough?

STOMIL: Not at all. Not for me. I'm the kind of man who goes deeper. If we're going to discuss this, we've got to take the imponderables into account.

ARTHUR: Oh Lord, Father, can't you button your fly first and then talk it over?

STOMIL: That would be a complete reversal of the logical thought process. The effect would precede the cause. Man should never act without thinking, never act like an automaton.

ARTHUR: I take it then that you will not button your pajamas.

STOMIL: No, son. Anyway, I can't. No buttons.

He takes a swallow of coffee. He sets the cup down on the table. Unnoticed, EDDIE *has crept up behind* ARTHUR.

ARTHUR: I might have expected as much.

STOMIL: Not at all. In this case at least, matter springs from the mind.

EDDIE *reaches over Arthur's shoulder for the cup and drinks.*

ARTHUR: That's precisely what I wanted to talk to you about, Father.

STOMIL: Later, boy. Later. (*Takes a swallow out of the cup which is now in front of* EDDIE. *Looks toward the catafalque.*) Isn't anybody ever going to remove that thing?

ELEANOR: Why?

STOMIL: Well, I have nothing against it on purely formal grounds. Actually it enriches reality, stimulates the imagination. But I could use the space for my experiments.

ELEANOR: But you've got the whole house.

EUGENIA: I'd be glad, too, if you got rid of it. Then Arthur couldn't torture me.

ARTHUR (*pounding the table with his fist*): You see? What's going on in this house? Chaos, anarchy, entropy! How long has it been since Grandfather died? Ten years!

And all that time nobody's ever thought of ridding the house of that catafalque. Incredible! We should be grateful, though, that you at least took Grandfather out of the house.

EUGENE: We couldn't keep Grandfather any longer.

ARTHUR: I'm not interested in the details. It's the principle of the thing.

STOMIL (*drinking coffee, bored*): Really?

ARTHUR (*jumps up and runs across the stage*): But it's not only Grandfather. I was born twenty-five years ago and my baby carriage is still standing here. (*He kicks the baby carriage.*) Why isn't it up in the attic? And what's this thing? Mother's wedding dress. (*He pulls the dusty veil from under a pile of rubbish.*) Why isn't it put away in a closet? And Uncle Eugene's riding breeches. What are they lying around here for when the last horse he ever rode died forty years ago? No order, no sense of reality, no decency, no initiative. You can't move in this place, you can't breathe, you can't live!

Taking advantage of the confusion, EDDIE empties the cup at one gulp.

ELEANOR (*aside to EDDIE*): How beautifully you drink, Eddie!

STOMIL: My boy, tradition doesn't interest me in the slightest. Your indignation is absurd. You know very well we attach no importance to these monuments of the past, these relics of family tradition. That's why everything's lying around like this. We live in freedom. (*He looks into the cup.*) Where's my coffee?

ARTHUR: No, no, Father, you just don't understand me. That's not what bothers me. No, that's not it.

STOMIL: Then kindly explain yourself more clearly, will you, boy? (*To* ELEANOR.) Isn't there any more coffee?

ELEANOR: No, there won't be any until the day after tomorrow.

STOMIL: Why the day after tomorrow?

ELEANOR: How should I know?

STOMIL: All right. Never mind.

ARTHUR: Listen to me! It's not this particular tradition that bothers me. It's a fact that in this family there's no frame of reference at all. All that's left is bits and pieces, fragments, rubbish. You've destroyed everything but you go on destroying; you've gone on so long you've finally forgotten why you began in the first place.

ELEANOR: He's right. Stomil, do you still remember how we shattered tradition? How, in protest against tradition, I gave myself to you with Mummy and Daddy looking on? In the first row of the orchestra at the opening night of *Tannhäuser*. What a gorgeous scandal that was! Where are the days when people were still shocked by such things? And then you proposed to me.

STOMIL: As I recall it was at the National Museum's first avant-garde exhibition. The critics gave us rave reviews.

ELEANOR: No. It was at the opera. At the exhibition it wasn't you, or maybe it wasn't me. You're getting everything mixed up.

STOMIL: Possibly. (*With enthusiasm.*) The days of revolt, the time of the great leap forward. Liberation from the fetters of the old art and the old way of life. Man coming into his own, man overthrowing the old gods and putting himself on the pedestal. The seed burst open, the chains snapped. Revolution and release. That was our slogan then. Away with outmoded forms, down with convention! Long live the dynamic! Life as creation, an incessant striving toward new frontiers! Movement and struggle! All form transcended!

ELEANOR: Stomil! You've been drinking at the fountain of youth! I hardly recognize you.

STOMIL: Yes, we were young once.

ELEANOR: What do you mean? We haven't grown any older. We've never betrayed our ideals. Why, even now our motto is still: Forward! Ever forward!

STOMIL (*without enthusiasm*): Yes. Yes. That's right.

ELEANOR: Do we have any prejudices? Do conventions mean anything to us? Aren't we still fighting against the old? Aren't we free?

STOMIL: The old what?

ELEANOR: Well, the old times. Don't you remember? Don't tell me you've forgotten what we were just talking about? All those fetters, those rusty chains of religion, morality, society, art. Especially art, Stomil. Art!

STOMIL: Yes, of course. But when was all that actually?

ELEANOR: Just a minute. Let me figure it out. We were married in 1900 . . . no, just let me think . . . Arthur was born in 1930, or . . . oh, be quiet, will you? Or was it 1940?

STOMIL: Oh, *then*. I see. (*He stops in front of the mirror, passes his hand over his face.*)

ELEANOR: Don't interrupt me. You're getting me all mixed up . . . (*Figures in an undertone, thoroughly absorbed.*) 1914 . . . 1918 . . . 1921 . . .

STOMIL (*at the mirror*): We're young. Eternally young . . .

ARTHUR: Father's right.

STOMIL: What do you mean?

ARTHUR: It's all dead and gone now. All in the past.

ELEANOR *runs across the stage, whispering dates, be-coming more and more entangled in her calculations.*

STOMIL: What's gone?

ARTHUR: All those fetters and chains! They're all gone now, unfortunately.

STOMIL: Unfortunately? You don't know what you're saying. If you'd lived in those days, you'd know how much we've done for you. You have no idea what the world was like then. Can you imagine how much courage it took to dance the tango? Do you realize that in those days there were hardly any fallen women? That the only recognized style of painting was naturalism? That the theater was utterly bourgeois? Stifling. Insufferable. You couldn't even put your elbows down on the dinner table! I can still remember a youth demonstration on that very issue. Why, it wasn't until after 1900 that the boldest, the most advanced spirits stopped giving up their seats to elderly people. No, we didn't spare ourselves in our struggle for these rights and if you today can push your grandmother around, its to us your thanks are due. You simply can't imagine how much you owe us. To think how we struggled to give you this freedom which you now despise!

ARTHUR: And what did you do with it? What did you produce? This bawdyhouse where nothing works because everyone can do what he pleases, where there are no laws and no violations?

STOMIL: I know only one law: Don't hesitate, do what you feel like. Every man is entitled to his own kind of happiness.

ELEANOR: Stomil, I've got it! I've figured it out! It was 1928.

STOMIL: What was?

ELEANOR (*in consternation*): I've forgotten.

ARTHUR: You've poisoned the generations before you and after you with your freedom. Look at Grandmother! She's completely addled. Haven't you noticed?

EUGENIA: I just knew he'd drag me into it.

STOMIL: There's nothing wrong with Mama. What do you mean?

ARTHUR: Naturally you're not shocked by her senile demoralization. Once she was a dignified, self-respecting grandmother. And now? Now she plays poker with Eddie!

EDDIE: I beg your pardon. We also play bridge, you know.

ARTHUR: I wasn't talking to you.

STOMIL: Each has the right to do what he wants and with whomever he chooses. Old people too.

ARTHUR: That's not a right. It's a moral obligation to be immoral.

STOMIL: You astonish me. Your opinions are so terribly outdated. When we were your age, we considered every kind of conformity disgraceful. Rebellion! Rebellion alone had any value for us.

ARTHUR: What value?

STOMIL: A dynamic and therefore positive value, though sometimes in a negative way. I trust you don't think we were merely blind anarchists? Certainly not. We were a column marching off to the future, a movement, a historical process. History is indebted to us. What is rebellion? The rock on which progress builds its temple and the greater the scope of the rebellion the grander the temple will be. Believe me: the scope of our rebellion was prodigious.

ARTHUR: But if that's the case . . . why these misunderstand-

ings? If you too are trying to do something construc-
tive, why can't we build together?

STOMIL: Impossible. What I said just now was purely objective. I described our historical role, but said nothing
of our intentions. Well then, what were our intentions? Why, to do what we wanted, go our own ways,
each for himself. We have always pursued our own in-
clinations. But by opposing everything, we paved the
way for the future.

ARTHUR: What future?

STOMIL: That's not my affair. My job was to shatter exist-
ing forms.

ARTHUR: In other words, we're still enemies?

STOMIL: Why take it so tragically? All you need to do
is stop worrying about principles.

ELEANOR: Yes. What I still can't understand is why you,
the youngest of us all, should be the one to harp on
principles. It used to be the other way around.

ARTHUR: Because I'm starting out in the world. But what a
world! If I want a world, I've got to make one.

STOMIL: But you're young, Arthur. Don't you want to be
modern? At your age?

ARTHUR: That's just the point. These modern times of
yours. Even Grandmother has grown old in this world
that has lost its standards. That's how modern your era
is. What's more, you've grown old in it.

EUGENE: If you'll allow me to put in a word, I should like
to call your attention to certain achievements, for instance, the right to wear short pants . . . ah, the fresh
feel of the breeze . . .

ARTHUR: Oh, keep quiet, Uncle. Don't you realize that,
precisely because everything is possible, nothing is
possible anymore? If you were at least bucking conven-

tion with your short pants. But all convention was broken ages ago. By the time you came along it was all taken care of. The whole thing is absurd.

STOMIL: Well, what *do* you want then? Tradition?

ARTHUR: An orderly world!

STOMIL: That's all?

ARTHUR: . . . and the right to rebel.

STOMIL: That's it. That's what I've been telling you all along: *rebel!*

ARTHUR: Don't you see that you've deprived me of every last chance to revolt? You've been nonconformists so long that there aren't any conventions left to rebel against. You've left nothing for me . . . nothing! Your only norm is the absence of all norms. The only thing left for me to rebel against is you . . . you and your immorality.

STOMIL: Go right ahead. Did I ever tell you not to?

EUGENE: That's the stuff, Arthur. You'll show them.

ELEANOR: Maybe it would calm you down. You've been so jittery lately. . . .

EUGENIA *makes signs to* EDDIE; *they come to an understanding behind Arthur's back and pick up the cards.*

ARTHUR (*falls into an armchair with resignation*): Impossible!

ELEANOR: Why?

EUGENE: We're all in favor of it.

ARTHUR: Rebel against you? What are you anyway? A formless mass, an amorphous blob, an atomized world, a mob without shape or structure. Your world can't even be blown up; it's disintegrated all by itself.

STOMIL: You mean we're no good for anything?

ARTHUR: Exactly.

ELEANOR: But couldn't you just try?

ARTHUR: There's nothing to try. It's hopeless. You're all so disgustingly tolerant.

STOMIL: Yes, that could be irritating, I suppose. Still, I don't like to see you feeling so left out.

ELEANOR (*stands behind him and strokes his hair*): Poor little Arthur. You mustn't think your mother's heart is made of stone.

EUGENE: We all love you, Arthur. We want to help you.

EUGENIA (*to* EDDIE): I pass.

ARTHUR: It's hopeless. This nonconformism you're pushing me into is only a new kind of conformism. But I can't be a conformist forever. I'm twenty-five. My friends are all laughing at me.

STOMIL: But what about art, Arthur? What about art?

ELEANOR: Exactly. You've taken the words out of my mouth.

ARTHUR: What art?

STOMIL: Well, art in general. I've devoted my whole life to art. Art is eternal rebellion. Why don't you give it a try?

EDDIE: Bring your bedding. Skip the wedding.

EUGENIA: Crash, smash, I'm out of cash.

ARTHUR: Father, you bore me. I want to be a doctor.

ELEANOR: A disgrace to the whole family! I've always dreamed of his becoming an artist. When I was carrying him in my womb, I ran through the woods stark naked, singing Bach. All for nothing!

ARTHUR: Maybe you sang out of tune.

STOMIL: All the same, don't give up hope. You still don't understand the value of art. I've just had an idea for a new experiment. You'll see.

ELEANOR (*clapping her hands*): Eugenia, Eddie. Stomil has come up with something new.

EUGENIA: Again?

STOMIL: Yes. It came to me this morning. It's absolutely original.

ELEANOR: You'll put it on right away, won't you, Stomil?

STOMIL: I'm ready.

EUGENE: Heaven help us!

ELEANOR: Eugene, move the table. Make room.

> EUGENE *shoves the table aside with a good deal of crashing and thumping.* EUGENIA *and* EDDIE *pick up the cards and step to one side. Under the mound of draperies suggesting a bed, something starts to move. Finally Cousin Ala's head comes to light.*

ALA (*a girl of eighteen with a good figure and long hair. She blinks in the light and yawns*): Where am I? First all that shouting and now they're moving furniture . . . What time is it anyway?

ARTHUR: Ala!

ELEANOR: I forgot to tell you, Ala has been here since six o'clock this morning.

STOMIL: This is marvelous, Ala. You're just in time for the show. (*To* EUGENE.) That's fine. Now the catafalque.

ARTHUR: But why didn't you tell me? If I'd known, I'd have kept them quiet.

> *He notices that* EDDIE *is approaching* ALA *with interest.*

Back Eddie. Face to the wall.

> EDDIE *steps back obediently and stands with his face to the wall.*

Did you sleep well?

ELEANOR: How did you do it, Stomil?

STOMIL: I unscrewed the fuse and fired the revolver.

ELEANOR: Marvelous!

EUGENE: What's so marvelous about it?

STOMIL: Don't you understand?

EUGENE: No, I don't.

ELEANOR: Don't mind him, Stomil. Eugene has always been slow.

STOMIL: How about you, Eugenia?

EUGENIA: Huh?

STOMIL (*louder*): Did you understand the experiment, Mama?

ELEANOR: The experiment has made her deaf.

EUGENE: That doesn't surprise me.

STOMIL: Let me explain. The shock method creates an immediate unity of action and perception. See?

EUGENE: Yes, but . . .

STOMIL: Yes, but what?

EUGENE: But what's that got to do with Adam and Eve?

ELEANOR: Eugene, do try to concentrate.

STOMIL: What we are dealing with here is an intrinsically theatrical phenomenon, the dynamics of sense perception. That means something to you, doesn't it?

EUGENE: Frankly, I don't think it does.

STOMIL (*throws the revolver on the catafalque*): I give up.

ELEANOR: Don't be discouraged, Stomil. Who's going to experiment if you lose heart?

All stand up and put the chairs back in their places.

EUGENE: A flop, friends.

EDDIE: Give me the movies.

ELEANOR: Well, now what should we do?

ARTHUR: Clear out! All of you. Out!

STOMIL: What's got into you?

ARTHUR: All of you! I can't bear the sight of you.

STOMIL: Is that a way to treat your own father?

ARTHUR: I used to have a father. Not anymore. I'll have to make myself a father.

STOMIL: You? *You* make *me?*

ARTHUR: You and the whole lot of you. I'm going to make you all over. And now get out. This minute!

STOMIL: That boy's going just a bit too far.

ELEANOR: Never mind, Stomil. Thank God, we're enlightened.

STOMIL: You think I should really go?

ELEANOR: Why not? After all, you're not really interested in anything but your experiments.

STOMIL: Ah yes, art! Modern art! Give me God and I'll make an experiment out of Him.

ELEANOR: There. You see!

They all go out through the door left rear.

EDDIE (*to* EUGENIA): Come on, Grandma.

EUGENIA: Don't forget the cards.

EDDIE picks up the cards and goes out with EUGENIA.

EDDIE (*turning around again, to* ARTHUR): If you need anything . . .

ARTHUR (*stamping his foot*): Get out!

EDDIE (*conciliatory*): Okay, okay!

He goes out left with EUGENIA.

EUGENE (*after making sure that the others are gone*): You're absolutely right, Arthur. Between you and me, they're a bad lot.

ARTHUR: You too. Out!

EUGENE: Certainly. Certainly, my boy. I'm going. I only wanted to tell you that you can count on me.

ARTHUR: What do you mean?

EUGENE: Never mind. Just do what you think right. But remember. I can be useful to you. I'm not as far gone as the rest of them. (*More softly.*) I'm an old-timer.

ARTHUR: Glad to hear it. But now leave us alone, will you?

EUGENE (*goes out left, turns around again and says with emphasis*): An old-timer. (*Exits.*)

ALA: Now what?

ARTHUR: Now I'll explain everything.

Stefan Schnabel as Stomil

Elizabeth Swain as Ala

Lilyan Wilbur as Eleanor, David Margulies as Arthur, Stefan Schnabel as Stomil, Elizabeth Swain as

ACT TWO

The same scene as in Act One. The only light comes from a simple standing lamp. ARTHUR *is sitting in an armchair. Someone enters from the right.*

ARTHUR: Who's there?

FIGURE: Me.

ARTHUR: Who's me?

FIGURE: Your Uncle Eugene.

ARTHUR: Password?

EUGENE: New life. Countersign?

ARTHUR: Rebirth. (*Pause.*) All right. Come in.

> EUGENE *steps into the light. He sits down facing* ARTHUR.

EUGENE: Oof. I'm exhausted.

ARTHUR: Is everything ready?

EUGENE: I've brought everything I could down from the attic. You should see the moths! You think it will work?

ARTHUR: It's got to work.

EUGENE: I'm worried, worried. They're so demoralized . . . Think of it. A whole lifetime in this bawdy-house . . . I beg your pardon, I meant this atmosphere of moral disintegration. You see, it's contagious. Forgive me.

ARTHUR: Forget it. What's my father doing?

EUGENE: He's in his room, working on a new production. Don't you feel sorry for him sometimes? After all, he actually believes in that art of his.

ARTHUR: Then why do you discourage him?

EUGENE: For spite. To get his goat. But the fact is, those experiments of his don't mean a thing to me. What do you make of them?

ARTHUR: I've got other problems. And Mother?

EUGENE *stands up, goes to the door left rear and looks through the keyhole.*

EUGENE: Can't see a thing. Either she's turned the light out or hung something over the keyhole. (*He goes back to his former place.*)

ARTHUR: And Grandmother Eugenia?

EUGENE: Probably sitting at her mirror, putting on makeup.

ARTHUR: Good. You may go now. I have an important appointment in a few minutes.

EUGENE (*stands up*): Any further orders?

ARTHUR: Be vigilant. Eyes open, mouth shut, and ready for action.

EUGENE: Yes, sir. (*On his way out.*) God protect you, Arthur, my boy . . . Maybe we'll manage to bring the good old days back again yet.

Goes out to the right. ALA *enters by way of the corridor right. She is still wearing her nightgown.*

ALA (*yawning*): What did you want me for?

ARTHUR: Shh . . . quiet.

ALA: Why?

ARTHUR: This is private—between you and me.

ALA: You think they care what we do? We could climb up the walls and sleep on the ceiling for all they care. (*She sits down, wincing as though in pain.*)

ARTHUR: What's wrong?

ALA: Stomil pinched me twice today.

ARTHUR: The rotter!

ALA: Arthur, he's your father!

ARTHUR (*kissing her hand gallantly*): Thank you for re-
minding me.

ALA: It sounds so old-fashioned, nobody calls his father a
rotter nowadays.

ARTHUR: What *do* you call him then?

ALA: Nothing. You just ignore him.

ARTHUR (*disappointed*): Then I was mistaken.

ALA: Well, it's your headache that he's your father. Per-
sonally, I think he's great.

ARTHUR (*contemptuously*): An artist!

ALA: What's wrong with that?

ARTHUR: Artists are a plague. They were the first to con-
taminate our society.

ALA (*bored*): Oh, who cares? (*Yawns.*) What did you
want me for? It's cold in here. I'm practically naked.
Hadn't you noticed?

ARTHUR: Well, what do you say? Have you thought it over?

ALA: You mean will I marry you? But I've already told you.
I don't see the point.

ARTHUR: You mean the answer is no?

ALA: Why do you get so worked up about it? I mean—I
don't care—if it means so much to you, we can get
married tomorrow. We're already cousins.

ARTHUR: But I *want* you to care! I want you to realize that
marriage is something very important.

ALA: Important? Why? I don't get it. If I'm going to have
a baby it'll be with you, not with the minister. So
what's the problem?

ARTHUR: Well, if it's not important in itself, then we've
got to make it important.

ALA: What for?

ARTHUR: Nothing is important in itself. Things in them-
selves are meaningless. Unless we give them character,
we drown in a sea of indifference. We have to create
meanings, because they don't exist in nature.

ALA: But what for? What for?

ARTHUR: Well if you must have a reason, let's say: for our
own pleasure and profit.

ALA: Pleasure?

ARTHUR: Yes. We derive pleasure from profit and we only
profit from doing things we attach importance to—
difficult things, the unusual things that seem rare and
precious. And that's why we have to create a system of
values.

ALA: Philosophy bores me. I think I prefer Stomil. (*She
sticks her leg out from under the nightgown.*)

ARTHUR: You only think that. Kindly remove that leg.

ALA: You don't like it?

ARTHUR: That has nothing whatsoever to do with the subject.

ALA (*obstinately*): You really don't like it?

ARTHUR (*with difficulty takes his eyes off her leg*): Oh, all
right, show your leg if you want to. Anyway, it only
proves my point.

ALA: My leg? (*She examines her leg closely.*)

ARTHUR: Yes. Do you know why you're showing your leg?
Because I don't leap all over you like my artist father
and everybody else does. That worries you. You were
pretty bewildered this morning when we were all
alone. You thought you knew what I wanted from you.

ALA: That's not true.

ARTHUR: Not true? Ha. You think I didn't see how upset
you were when I proposed marriage instead of just
picking you up and throwing you down on the bed?

ALA: I had a headache.

ARTHUR: Headache? Go on. You just couldn't figure out *what* was going on. You thought I wasn't attracted, that you must be losing your charms. If I suddenly started acting like my father, it would be a relief, wouldn't it? Yes. Except you'd run away, just to get even with me.

ALA (*stands up with dignity*): I'm running all right.

ARTHUR (*takes her by the hand and pulls her down into the chair*): Sit down. I haven't finished yet. All you care about is your sex appeal. You're so primitive! You can't think about anything else. You don't know anything else!

ALA: Are you suggesting that I'm backward? (*She tries again to stand up.*)

ARTHUR (*holding her down*): You stay right here. You've confirmed my theory. My behavior was atypical; that baffled you. The unusual is a value in itself. See? I have given meaning to an encounter that would otherwise have meant nothing. I!

ALA: Well, if you're so terribly clever, what do you need me for? If you're so awfully superior, why don't you just live all by yourself?

ARTHUR: You don't have to be so touchy.

ALA: We'll see how far you get alone. Or with Uncle Eugene. (*She resolutely draws her nightgown over her knees, buttons it up to the neck, and wraps herself in a steamer rug. She puts on the bowler and draws it down deep over her forehead.*)

ARTHUR (*shyly*): Don't be angry.

ALA: What do you care?

Pause.

ARTHUR: Aren't you too warm . . . in that blanket?

ALA: No.

ARTHUR: Uncle Eugene's hat doesn't look very good on you.

ALA: I don't care.

ARTHUR: Suit yourself. Where were we anyway? Oh yes, a system of values . . . (*He moves his chair closer to* ALA.) Now, generally speaking, a system of values is indispensable to the proper functioning both of the individual and of society. (*He seizes Ala's hand.*) Without the right kind of values we can never hope to create a harmonious world or establish the necessary balance between those elements commonly termed good and evil—though of course I use these words in their larger rather than strictly ethical sense. Now in this connection our task is two-fold: We must, one, restore the practical relevance of these concepts and, two, formulate rules of conduct which . . .

He flings himself at ALA *and tries to kiss her. She struggles free; they wrestle.* EDDIE *enters with his towel around his neck and a hairnet on his head.*

EDDIE (*with the pretentious enunciation typical of the semi-literate*): Oh, do excuse me.

ARTHUR (*lets* ALA *go as if nothing had happened.* ALA *straightens her hat and rubs her shoulder demonstratively*): What are *you* doing here?

EDDIE: I was just going to the kitchen for a drink of water. I beg your pardon, I didn't know you were conversing.

ARTHUR: Water? Water? What for?

EDDIE (*with dignity*): Because I'm thirsty, sir.

ARTHUR: At this hour? In the middle of the night?

EDDIE (*offended*): If that's the way you feel about it, I can go without.

ARTHUR (*furious*): Drink and get out!

EDDIE: As you wish. (*He goes majestically to the door left rear.*)

ARTHUR: Just a minute.

EDDIE: Yes, sir?

ARTHUR: The kitchen is on the right.

EDDIE: There? Impossible.

ARTHUR: I believe I know where the kitchen is in my own house.

EDDIE: You just can't be sure of anything these days. (*He changes his direction and goes out through the door right rear.*)

ARTHUR: That idiot! I'll have to take care of him once and for all.

ALA (*icily*): Have you finished taking care of me?

ARTHUR: It's all his fault.

ALA: I suppose it was his fault you nearly twisted my arm off.

ARTHUR: Does it hurt very much?

ALA: What do you care?

She affects a cry of pain. ARTHUR, *troubled, tries to examine her shoulder.*

ARTHUR: Where does it hurt? (*He touches her shoulder, but not with his original purpose.*)

ALA (*uncovering her shoulder*): Here . . .

ARTHUR: I'm terribly sorry.

ALA (*uncovering her back*): . . . and here . . .

ARTHUR (*dismayed*): Really, I didn't mean to . . .

ALA (*thrusts her leg forward*): . . . and here . . .

ARTHUR: How can I ever make it up to you? . . .

ALA (*lays her forefinger on her rib*): . . . and here too!

ARTHUR: Forgive me. I didn't mean to . . .

ALA: Now you've shown what you really are—a brute. First a lot of talk and then the usual. (*She sinks tragically into an armchair.*) We poor women! Is it our fault we have bodies? If we could only check them somewhere like a hat or a coat. Then maybe we'd be safe from our sweet-talking cousins. Frankly, I'm surprised. You with your noble ideals.

ARTHUR (*confused*): But really, I . . .

ALA: No excuses! You don't think I like a good conversation too? But that calls for a nice restful atmosphere. How can I converse when some philosopher is clutching at my legs? But never mind. What were we talking about? It was just beginning to be interesting when you . . .

Behind the door through which EDDIE *has passed a sound of gushing water is heard. Then gargling.*

ARTHUR: This is too much. Do you seriously think I wanted to rape you?

ALA (*alarmed*): Didn't you?

ARTHUR: Certainly not. I was only teaching you a lesson.

ALA: Thanks. I know that subject.

ARTHUR: You can only think about one thing. Then why did you resist? Come on. Why?

ALA: You're vulgar.

ARTHUR: Science knows no shame. Why?

ALA: Well, why did you attack me?

ARTHUR: Attack you? I was sacrificing myself.

ALA: What?

ARTHUR: Yes, sacrificing myself in my effort to make certain things clear to you. It was a pure exercise in sexual pragmatics.

ALA: Pig! Scientific pig! Pragmatics? What is it anyway?

Some new kind of perversion?

ARTHUR: There's nothing new about it. I'm sure we'll always be friends. Yes, women will follow me.

ALA: Women? Which women?

ARTHUR: All women. Women throughout the world will be my allies. And once the women are convinced, the men will soon come around.

ALA: What women? Anybody I know? Anyway, do what you like with them. I couldn't care less.

ARTHUR: Look here. The central fact of history is the total enslavement of women, children and artists by men.

ALA: I thought you didn't approve of artists.

ARTHUR: That's beside the point. The reason men don't like artists is that artists aren't men. That's what has always brought artists and women together—unfortunately. The ideas men have dreamed up—like honor, logic, progress—have always been foreign to women and artists. It's only very recently that the male has even begun to suspect the existence of such things as ambiguity, relativity, forgetfulness—in short, the glamor and poetry of this world, the exact opposite of what he had originally invented in that thick soldier's skull of his and tried to impose on women, children and artists.

ALA: But what about you? Aren't you a male?

ARTHUR: I transcend myself; I take an objective view. That's essential if I'm to carry out my plan.

ALA: Can I trust you?

ARTHUR: It was only to make up for their lack of imagination that men invented the concept of honor. And, at the same time, of effeminacy. Why? To guarantee male solidarity. Anyone who dared question the code of manly virtues was immediately accused of being effeminate. The result was that, in self-defense, women, children and artists closed ranks to form a single community. They had no choice. . . . Just a second.

The gargling is still heard from the kitchen. ARTHUR *goes to the kitchen door.*

ALA: Maybe he's washing.

ARTHUR: Him? Not likely! (*He goes back to his place.*) Let's get back to the subject.

ALA: I just don't believe you. I see what you're getting at. You can't fool me.

ARTHUR: I have no desire to fool you. I'm simply trying to make you aware of your own interests as a woman.

ALA: What does that mean? You want me to strip?

ARTHUR: Oh, don't be tedious. Once you've finally come to see that our interests coincide, you'll be willing to work with me. What do men want? They want to abolish all conventions relating to sex. And why? To make life easier for *them*, to do away with all barriers between desire and satisfaction.

ALA: You've got something there. They jump you like a bull. Like you did just now.

ARTHUR: I can't deny that as an individual I'm subject to natural drives. But I have a higher goal. Taking advantage of the general breakdown in values, men have done everything they could to do away with the last remaining rules governing sexual behavior. I can't believe that women really like it, and that's the basis of my plan.

ALA: I like it fine.

ARTHUR: That's a lie. You *can't*.

ALA: Yes, I like it. It means I'm free, I can do as I please. For instance, if I take my clothes off right now, what can you do about it? (*She throws off the steamer rug and removes her hat.*)

ARTHUR: Stop it. This is a serious discussion.

ALA (*undoing the ribbons of her nightgown*): Why should I? Who's going to stop me? You? My mother? God? (*She bares her shoulders.*)

ARTHUR: Cover yourself this minute! Pull up that nightgown. (*He tries desperately to look away.*)

ALA: I will not. It's my nightgown.

Eddie's head is seen in the doorway.

Oh, hi, Eddie. Come on in.

ARTHUR (*pushing* EDDIE *away*): Get out or I'll kill you. Taking your clothes off in front of this . . . Have you no shame?

ALA: He may not be very cultured, but he has marvelous eyes.

ARTHUR: Eyes like a pig.

ALA: *I* like them.

ARTHUR: I'll kill him.

ALA (*sweetly*): You wouldn't be jealous by any chance?

ARTHUR: I am not jealous.

ALA: First he's brutal. Then he's jealous. You ought to be ashamed of yourself.

ARTHUR (*furious, face to face with* ALA): Go on then. Undress! I'm not stopping you.

ALA: I don't feel like it anymore.

ARTHUR: Suit yourself.

ALA (*retreating*): I've changed my mind.

ARTHUR (*following her*): Oh, you don't feel like it anymore? Tell me, why don't you want to anymore! Tell me why you wanted to before.

ALA: My God, what a lunatic!

ARTHUR (*seizes her by the arm*): Why?

ALA: I don't know.

ARTHUR: Tell me!

ALA: What should I say? I don't know, I just don't know. Let me go.

ARTHUR (*letting her go*): You know perfectly well. It's because you only pretend to like all this absence of rules, this debauchery, this promiscuity.

ALA: Oh, I only pretend, do I?

ARTHUR: Of course. You really hate it, because it's not to your advantage. This lack of forms and norms cuts down your freedom of choice. There's nothing left for you to do but take off your clothes and put them back on again.

ALA: That's not true.

ARTHUR: Then why this sudden modesty?

Pause.

ALA: Now you're being logical. You just said that logic was nonsense.

ARTHUR: I said that?

ALA: Yes, only a minute ago. I heard you.

ARTHUR (*disgruntled*): You must have heard wrong.

ALA: I heard you quite clearly.

ARTHUR: Well, let's not bicker. But I still don't believe you. I'm convinced that the convention of unconventionality goes against your grain. You didn't make it up.

ALA: Who did then?

ARTHUR: Men! You only pretend to like it. And now you're stuck with it, and nobody likes to admit he's just following the herd.

ALA: But if I don't like it why should I go along with it?

ARTHUR: For fear of losing your attractiveness. To keep up with the fashion. Admit it!

ALA: No.

ARTHUR: No? All right. At least you admit there's something to admit. Come on. Why all these lies? Can't you see that important issues are at stake? I simply refuse to believe that you want to go to bed with every man in the world. Wanting to attract them is something else again. You want to be able to choose for yourself. But how can a woman choose when there are no conventions? Tell me that.

ALA: I'm free. I know exactly what I want.

ARTHUR: But you're weak by nature. What chance do you have when you're all alone with a strange man who's stronger than you and there's no convention to protect you? Let's assume, for instance, that you don't care for me. If Eddie hadn't butted in, you'd have been sunk, because I'm the stronger.

ALA: I could always take up judo.

ARTHUR: You take everything so literally. Can't you women ever understand a general idea?

ALA: Lots of girls study judo. I'd have you begging for mercy.

ARTHUR: Excellent. You're getting there. You're coming around. Don't you see? Why does it have to be judo when conventions are quite effective? I'd be kneeling at your feet with a bouquet in my hand begging you to take pity on me, to grant me a ray of hope. Behind a solid wall of conventions, without any wrestling, without even getting your hair mussed, you'd have me at your mercy. Wouldn't that be better than judo?

ALA: You really mean it? Down on your knees?

ARTHUR: Certainly.

ALA: Okay. Go ahead.

ARTHUR: Go ahead and what?

ALA: Down on your knees!

ARTHUR: Impossible.

ALA (*disappointed*): Why?

ARTHUR: Because there are no conventions left. Now do you see what a fix you're in?

ALA: Isn't there anything we can do about it?

ARTHUR: Yes.

ALA: What?

ARTHUR: Establish new conventions or bring back the old ones. And that's exactly what I'm going to do—with your help. Everything's prepared. All I need is your help.

ALA: Great! And you'll really get down on your knees?

ARTHUR: I will.

ALA: All right. Now what can I do to help?

ARTHUR: Marry me. That's the first step. No more promiscuity, no more *dolce vita*. A real marriage. Not just dropping into city hall between breakfast and lunch. A genuine old-fashioned wedding with an organ playing and bridesmaids marching down the aisle. I'm especially counting on the procession. It will take them by surprise. That's the whole idea. And, from then on, they won't have time to think, to organize resistance and spread defeatism. It's the first shot that counts. Catching them off guard like that, we can force them to accept conventions they'll never break out of again. It's going to be the kind of wedding they'll have to take part in, and on my terms. I'll turn them into a bridal procession, and at long last my father will be forced to button his fly. What do you say?

ALA: And I'll get to wear a white wedding gown?

ARTHUR: White as snow. Everything strictly according to the rules. And at the same time you'll be helping all the women in the world. The rebirth of convention will set them free. What used to be the first rule of every encounter between a man and a woman? Conversation. A man couldn't get what he wanted just by making inarticulate sounds. He couldn't just grunt, he had to talk. And while he was talking, you—the woman—sat there demurely, sizing your opponent up. You let him talk and he showed his hand. Listening serenely, you drew up your own order of battle. Observing his tactics, you planned your own accordingly. Free to maneuver, you were always in command of the situation. You had time to think before coming to a decision and you could drag things out as long as you wanted. Even if he gnashed his teeth and secretly wished you in the bottom of hell, you knew he would never dare hit you. Up to the very last minute you could move freely, securely, triumphantly. Once you were engaged, you were safe, and even then traditional avenues of escape were open to you. Such were the blessings of conversation! But nowadays? Nowadays a man doesn't even have to introduce himself—and you will admit it's handy to know who a man is and what he does for a living.

EDDIE *tiptoes from the kitchen door to the door right. As he disappears in the doorway,* ARTHUR *sees him and goes after him.*

ALA: Was somebody listening?

ARTHUR (*coming back*): No.

ALA: I had the feeling there was.

ARTHUR: Let's settle this matter once and for all. Do you consent?

ALA: I don't know yet.

ARTHUR: You don't know? You mean I haven't convinced you?

ALA: Yes.

ARTHUR: Yes? Then you consent?

ALA: No . . .

ARTHUR: Yes or no?

ALA: I've got to think about it.

ARTHUR: But what is there to think about? It's as plain as day. I've got to rebuild a world, and for that I must have a wedding. It's perfectly simple. What don't you understand?

ALA: The whole thing, I guess.

ARTHUR: What do you mean?

ALA: Wait . . . Give me time.

ARTHUR: No, I can't wait. There just isn't time. I'll stay here while you go think it over. When you've made up your mind, come back and give me your answer. It's sure to be yes. I've explained everything.

ALA: And you really have nothing else to say? There's really nothing else you want to tell me?

ARTHUR: Run along now. I'll see you later.

ALA: You're throwing me out?

ARTHUR: No, I have a little private business to attend to.

ALA: Can't I stay?

ARTHUR: No. This is a family matter.

ALA: All right. Then I'll have my little secrets too. Just wait. You'll see.

ARTHUR (*impatiently*): Yes, yes, but run along now. Remember, I'll be waiting for you here.

ALA *goes out right.* ARTHUR *listens at the door left rear, and then goes to the door in the corridor. He knocks softly.*

STOMIL'S VOICE: Who's there?

ARTHUR (*rather softly*): Me. Arthur.

STOMIL: What do you want?

ARTHUR: Father, I've got to talk to you.

STOMIL: At this time of night? I'm busy. Come back tomorrow.

ARTHUR: It's urgent.

Pause.

STOMIL: But I've already told you, I'm busy. You can speak to me tomorrow.

ARTHUR *tries the door and sees that it is locked. He shoves with his shoulder.* STOMIL *opens. He is in pajamas as usual.*

Are you mad? What's going on?

ARTHUR (*in an ominous whisper*): Not so loud, Father.

STOMIL (*whispering, too, in spite of himself*): Why aren't you in bed?

ARTHUR: I can't sleep. It's time to take action.

STOMIL: In that case, good night.

He starts for his room. ARTHUR *holds him back.*

ARTHUR: I only wanted to ask you, Father, doesn't it bother you?

STOMIL: What?

ARTHUR: This thing with Eddie.

STOMIL: Eddie? Oh yes, I remember the man.

ARTHUR: What do you think of him?

STOMIL: He's amusing.

ARTHUR: Amusing? He's repulsive.

STOMIL: Oh I wouldn't say that. Eddie's an unusual type. A very modern, very authentic type.

ARTHUR: Is that all you have to say about him?

STOMIL: You see, our trouble is that we're still too conscious, too cerebral. Enslaved by centuries of culture.

Of course we've been doing our best to throw culture off, but we're still a long way from nature. But Eddie's lucky. He was born with what the rest of us can acquire only by art and effort. He interests me as an artist. I admire him the way a painter admires a landscape.

ARTHUR: Some landscape!

STOMIL: But don't you know there's been a complete revolution in aesthetics and morality. You keep making me remind you of things that ought to be self-evident. If Eddie shocks us now and then, it's because we're decadent. Sometimes I can't help feeling guilty toward Eddie. But I fight it down. We've got to get rid of these atavistic attitudes.

ARTHUR: And that's all you have to say?

STOMIL: I've been perfectly frank with you.

ARTHUR: Then I'll have to start all over again. Why do you tolerate him in your house?

STOMIL: Why not? He enriches our environment, he gives it a new tone, he adds a dash of authenticity. He even stimulates my imagination. We artists need an exotic touch now and then.

ARTHUR: Then you really don't know?

STOMIL: No, I don't know a thing.

ARTHUR: You're lying. You know perfectly well.

STOMIL: I repeat—I don't know. I don't want to know.

ARTHUR: He sleeps with Mother.

STOMIL *starts pacing.*

What do you say to that?

STOMIL: My dear boy. Let's assume what you say is true. Sexual freedom is the cornerstone of human freedom. What do *you* say to that?

ARTHUR: But it's the truth! They *do* sleep together!

STOMIL: I said we'd assume it's true. What follows? Nothing.

ARTHUR: Then you insist on treating it as an abstract hypothesis?

STOMIL: Why not? I'm a modern man. On the intellectual plane we can envisage any hypothesis, even the most ticklish. Without such hypotheses human thought would mark time. So do speak freely. I trust we can discuss this business without prudery. Now, what's your opinion?

ARTHUR: My opinion? I haven't got any opinion and I refuse to treat this matter as a theoretical exercise. This isn't a philosophical problem. It's the naked truth. Can't you see that? It's life. They've put horns on you. Long ones! And arguing isn't going to make them go away.

STOMIL: Horns! Horns! Horns are a primitive image, not an instrument of analysis. (*Nervously.*) Let's not descend to that low level.

ARTHUR: Father, you're a cuckold.

STOMIL: Hold your tongue. I forbid you to talk to me like that.

ARTHUR: You can't stop me. You're a cuckold.

STOMIL: I don't believe it.

ARTHUR: Ha! Now I've got you where I want you. Want me to prove it? Open that door. (*He points to the door left rear.*)

STOMIL: No!

ARTHUR: Are you afraid? Of course it's easier to perform theatrical experiments. When it comes to experiments you're a giant. In real life you're a midget.

STOMIL: Me?

ARTHUR: A hero in pajamas! A pint-sized Agamemnon!

STOMIL: I'll show you. You say they're in there?

ARTHUR: Look for yourself.

STOMIL: I'll show them. I'll show you. I'll show the whole lot of you! (*He runs to the door, stops.*) Or you know what I'll do? I'll take care of this whole thing tomorrow. (*He turns around.*)

ARTHUR (*barring the way*): No you won't. You're going in there right now.

STOMIL: Tomorrow! Or by mail. A letter. What do you say?

ARTHUR: Phony!

STOMIL: What did you say?

ARTHUR *makes horns on his forehead and laughs sardonically.*

All right then. Here I go!

ARTHUR (*stops him*): Just a second.

STOMIL (*with a martial air*): Let me at them.

ARTHUR: You'd better take this.

He takes the revolver which STOMIL *had left on the catafalque in Act One and gives it to his father.*

STOMIL: What's that?

ARTHUR: You can't go in there bare-handed.

Pause.

STOMIL (*calmly*): Now I see through you.

ARTHUR (*pushing him toward the door*): Get in there! There's not a minute to lose.

STOMIL (*tearing himself loose*): Now I understand. You want a tragedy!

ARTHUR (*retreating*): A tragedy? What do you mean?

STOMIL: So that's what you're after, you dim little runt of a brainstorm, you . . .

ARTHUR: What are you trying . . .

STOMIL (*throwing the revolver on the table*): You want me to kill him? And then her? And then myself? Right?

ARTHUR: Of course not. I was only joking. I just thought that in case Eddie . . . he might do anything.

STOMIL: You'd love that, wouldn't you! The injured husband wiping out his shame in blood. Where do you *get* such ideas? From romantic novels?

ARTHUR: Father, you know I never . . .

STOMIL: I always knew the younger generation cared more about ideas than life, but I never expected my own son to sacrifice his father to an idea. Sit down!

ARTHUR *sits down obediently.*

That's it. Now we'll have a little talk. You want to bring back the old values. What for? Well, never mind that. That's your business. I've let you talk, I've heard you out, but now you're going just a bit too far. How fiendishly clever! So you need a tragedy! Tragedy has always been the most perfect expression of a society with established values. So you needed a tragedy and thought you'd drag me into it. Instead of the art form—which demands time and effort—you wanted the thing itself. Or, never mind if somebody's killed, never mind if your own father goes off to prison. No, all you care about is your idea. Do you want to know what I think of you? A formalist. A vulgar formalist. That's what you are. Your father and mother mean nothing to you. We can all die as long as form wins out. And the worst of it is that you don't even care about yourself. You're a fanatic!

ARTHUR: Maybe my motives aren't as formal as you think.

STOMIL: You dislike Eddie?

ARTHUR: I hate him.

STOMIL: Why? Eddie is necessity. He's the pure truth we've
 been searching for so long because we always thought
 it was somewhere else. Eddie is a fact. You can't hate
 facts. You've got to accept them.

ARTHUR: What do you want me to do, hug him?

STOMIL: Good Lord! You talk like a petulant child. I can
 only see one explanation. Maybe you've got an
 Oedipus.

ARTHUR: A what?

STOMIL: An Oedipus complex. Have you consulted an
 analyst?

ARTHUR: No. Mother's wonderful, but that's not it.

STOMIL: Too bad. Then at least we'd know where we were at.
 Anything is better than sheer lunacy. I guess you're
 just a formalist.

ARTHUR: I am not.

STOMIL: Oh yes you are. And an insufferable and dangerous
 one at that.

ARTHUR: It may look that way to you, but the truth is that
 I . . . I just can't go on like this. I can't live with you
 people.

STOMIL: I see. That's more like it. In other words, you're
 an egoist.

ARTHUR: Call it whatever you like. That's the way I am,
 that's all.

STOMIL: But suppose you succeeded in making me kill him,
 in packing me off to prison for life, what good would
 that do you?

ARTHUR: Something would be accomplished. Something
 tragic. You're right. Please forgive me. Tragedy is a
 form so vast and powerful that reality can never escape
 its grip.

STOMIL: You poor devil. You really believe that? Don't

you realize that tragedy isn't possible anymore? Reality
erodes all forms and that goes for tragedy too. Suppose
I actually killed him. What would be the good of it?

ARTHUR: It would be something irrevocable, masterful,
classical.

STOMIL: Not for a minute. It would be a farce. In our time
only farce is possible. A corpse won't change anything.
Why can't you face facts? Actually, a farce can be very
nice too.

ARTHUR: Not for me.

STOMIL: Lord, you can be stubborn!

ARTHUR: I can't help it. I've got to find a way out.

STOMIL: Regardless of reality?

ARTHUR: Yes. At any cost.

STOMIL: That's not so easy. I'd like to help you, but I
don't see how.

ARTHUR: Couldn't we give it a try?

STOMIL: Give what a try?

ARTHUR (*pointing to the door left rear*): With them.

STOMIL: You still have illusions?

ARTHUR: Even if you're right about farce . . . (*Gradually he
resumes his aggressiveness.*) It's only because you
people are such cowards. You complain, but you're
stuck in a farce because no one has the courage to
rebel. Why can't you free yourself by one act of sheer
violence? You're so logical, so analytical, you see everything in the abstract. Instead of changing anything,
you make diagrams. You've come a long way, but what
have you actually done? Sat in a chair and discussed.
But this situation calls for action. If tragedy has become extinct it's only because you don't believe in it.
You and your damned compromises.

STOMIL: But why should we believe in tragedy? Come here,

son. I want to tell you something. All right. Eleanor is unfaithful to me with Eddie. What's so bad about that?

ARTHUR: But, Father, don't you know?

STOMIL: So help me, when you come right down to it, I don't. Maybe you can explain.

ARTHUR: I've never been in such a situation . . .

STOMIL: Try.

ARTHUR: It's obvious . . . Let me think . . .

STOMIL: Think away. Actually, I'd be delighted if you could convince me.

ARTHUR: Really?

STOMIL: To tell you the truth, I don't much care for this kind of thing either. In fact, I detest it. Only the more I think about it, the less I know why.

ARTHUR: So if I could convince you . . .

STOMIL: . . . I'd be very grateful.

ARTHUR: And you'd . . .

STOMIL: Go in and make a scene they'd remember as long as they lived. But I need a rational justification.

ARTHUR: Then you'd go in? Without being pushed?

STOMIL: I'd be delighted to. I've had it in for that bastard a long time. Believe it or not, nothing would please me doesn't tell me why.

more than to settle his hash. Except that my reason

ARTHUR: Father, let me hug you.

They hug each other.

To hell with reason!

STOMIL: But what can we do? It won't let go of us. You were talking about compromise. It's reason that makes us compromise.

ARTHUR: Well, then, Father, shall we give it a try? What

have we got to lose? If the worst comes to the worst, you'll shoot him.

STOMIL: Think so? If I could only be sure.

ARTHUR: Certainty comes later. The main thing now is to make up your mind.

STOMIL: Hm. Maybe you're right.

ARTHUR: I know I'm right. You'll see. We'll have our tragedy!

STOMIL: You've given me back my strength. The enthusiasm of youth untrammeled by the skepticism of the times. Ah, youth, youth!

ARTHUR: Shall we go in?

STOMIL: Yes. With you beside me, I feel better.

They stand up.

ARTHUR: Just one more thing. Give up those experiments of yours, will you? They only speed up the process of disintegration.

STOMIL: Well, but what can we do? Tragedy impossible, farce a bore—what's left but experiments?

ARTHUR: They only make things worse. Give them up, Father.

STOMIL: I don't know . . .

ARTHUR: Promise.

STOMIL: Later. Now we go in.

ARTHUR *puts the revolver back into Stomil's hand.*

ARTHUR: I'll wait here. If you need any help, just shout.

STOMIL: That won't be necessary. If anybody yells, it'll be him, not me.

ARTHUR: Father, I've always had confidence in you.

STOMIL: With good reason, my boy. I was the best shot in my regiment. Farewell! (*He goes to the door right rear.*)

ARTHUR: No, that's the kitchen.

STOMIL (*irresolute*): I could use a drink.

ARTHUR: Later. When it's all over. No time now.

STOMIL: Right! I'll kill him on the spot. (*He goes to the left-hand door, puts his hand on the knob.*) That scoundrel! Now he's going to pay!

He enters the room cautiously, closes the door behind him. ARTHUR *waits tensely. Total silence.* ARTHUR *paces nervously back and forth. Grows more and more impatient. Looks at his watch. Finally he makes a decision and flings both wings of the door open, so that the whole room can be seen. Under a bright, low-hanging lamp* ELEANOR, EDDIE, EUGENIA *and* STOMIL *are sitting at a round table, playing cards.*

ARTHUR: What's Eddie doing here? Why isn't Eddie . . . ?

STOMIL: Shhh! Take it easy, boy!

ELEANOR: Oh, it's you, Arthur? Are you still up?

EUGENIA: I told you he'd find us. He sticks his nose into everything.

ARTHUR: Father! . . . You . . . with them!

STOMIL: That's how it worked out . . . It's not *my* fault.

ELEANOR: Stomil turned up just in time. We needed a fourth.

ARTHUR: Father, how could you!

STOMIL: I told you it would end in a farce.

EDDIE: Your play, Mr. Stomil. What you got?

STOMIL: Here you are. (*To* ARTHUR.) A harmless pastime. You see the situation. What could I do?

ARTHUR: But, Father, you promised!

STOMIL: I promised nothing. We'll just have to wait.

ELEANOR: Instead of talking so much, would you please put your mind on the game, Stomil?

ARTHUR: For shame!

EUGENIA (*throws down her cards*): I simply can't play under these conditions. Can't anybody throw this little twerp out of here?

EDDIE: Easy, Grandma. Take it easy.

ELEANOR: Arthur, you ought to be ashamed, upsetting your grandmother like this.

EUGENIA: I told you we should lock the door. He's always looking for some way to pester me. You'll see. He'll put me back up on the catafalque!

ELEANOR: Oh, no he won't! We've got to finish this rubber first.

ARTHUR (*pounding the table with his fist*): Stop it!

ELEANOR: But we've just started.

EDDIE: You'd better listen to your mother. She's right. Look at the score cards, they're practically blank.

ARTHUR (*tearing the cards out of their hands*): Now you listen to me! I've got something to tell you. Now! This minute!

STOMIL: But Arthur, that was strictly between the two of us. Don't shout it from the rooftops.

ARTHUR: I pleaded with you. You wouldn't listen. Now I'm going to use force. Stop the game!

ELEANOR: What's going on?

EDDIE: What's got into you anyway? If I were your father, know what I'd do? I'd give you a good hiding.

ARTHUR: You shut up. (*Calmly but firmly.*) Father, the revolver.

EDDIE: A guy can still make a joke, can't he?

ELEANOR: A revolver? For God's sake, Stomil, don't give it to him. Talk to him. Do *something*. After all, you're his father.

STOMIL (*trying to take a severe tone*): Now see here,

Arthur, you're not a child. I'm sorry to have to speak to you like this, but . . .

ARTHUR *takes the revolver from Stomil's pajama pocket. All jump up.*

EUGENIA: He's gone mad. Stomil, why on earth did you make this child? Criminal negligence—that's what I call it.

EDDIE: Look here, Mr. Arthur . . .

ARTHUR: Silence! Into the living room, everybody.

One after another they go to the center of the stage. ARTHUR *remains standing at the door. As* STOMIL *passes him.*

I'll talk to you later.

STOMIL: What's wrong? I did my best.

ARTHUR: Your best!

EUGENIA *sits down on the sofa,* ELEANOR *in an armchair.* EDDIE *stands in the corner, takes a comb from his back pocket and runs it nervously through his hair.*

STOMIL (*facing* ELEANOR, *raises his arms*): I did everything I could to quiet him down. You saw me . . .

ELEANOR: Idiot. And you call yourself a father. Oh, if I were only a man!

STOMIL: That's easier said than done.

EUGENE *runs in.*

EUGENE (*to* ARTHUR): Has it started yet?

ARTHUR: Not yet. I'm still waiting for an answer.

EUGENE: I thought it had started. I heard a noise and I came running.

ARTHUR: That's all right. I'm glad you've come. Stay here and keep an eye on them. I'll be back in a second.

He gives him the revolver.

EUGENE: Yes, sir.

ELEANOR: Am I dreaming?

ARTHUR (*to* EUGENE): Don't let anybody make a move.

EUGENE: Yes, sir.

ELEANOR: Have you both gone mad?

ARTHUR: If anybody does move, shoot to kill. Understand?

EUGENE: Yes, sir.

ELEANOR: It's a plot! Mama, your brother's a gangster!

EUGENIA: Eugene, do put that thing away. People don't play cowboys at your age. (*She starts to stand up.*)

EUGENE: Stay where you are!

EUGENIA (*astonished*): Eugene, it's me—your sister Eugenia.

EUGENE: When I'm on duty, I have no sister.

EUGENIA: What duty? Don't be a fool.

EUGENE: I have enlisted in the service of an ideal!

ARTHUR: Splendid. I see I can rely on you. I'm going to leave you for a moment.

STOMIL: But, Arthur, can't you tell me, at least, what's going on? I thought we'd just become friends.

ARTHUR: I'll tell you everything in due time.

He goes out. EUGENE *sits down with his back to the wall, holding his revolver in readiness. He aims it vaguely but menacingly at each in turn.*

ELEANOR (*after a pause*): So that's it . . . Eugene, you've betrayed us.

EUGENE: Silence! (*Then justifying himself.*) That's not true I haven't betrayed anybody.

ARTHUR'S VOICE (*off*): Ala! Ala!

ELEANOR: You've betrayed your generation.

EUGENE: No, you're the traitors. You've all betrayed our good old days. I'm the only one who hasn't.

ARTHUR'S VOICE (*off*): Ala! Ala!

ELEANOR: All you are is the tool of a mad pack of young zealots. With a missionary complex. You think you're so clever. They'll use you and then kick you out like a dog.

EUGENE: We'll see who uses whom. I've been waiting a long time for someone like Arthur to come along.

ELEANOR: Now at least you've shown who you really are. All these years you've been wearing a mask, you hypocrite.

EUGENE: Yes, I have. And all these years I've suffered. I hated you for your degradation but I kept quiet because I had to, because you were the stronger. Now at last I can tell you what I think of you! What a pleasure!

ELEANOR: What are you going to do to us?

EUGENE: We're going to give you back your dignity. We're going to turn you degenerates back into human beings with decent principles—that's what we're going to do.

ELEANOR: By force?

EUGENE: If we can't do it any other way, yes.

STOMIL: This is a counter-reformation.

EUGENE: But for you it's salvation.

STOMIL: Salvation? From what?

EUGENE: From your damnable, diabolical freedom.

ARTHUR (*enters*): Uncle!

EUGENE: Sir?

ARTHUR: She's gone.

EUGENE: Look for her. She must be somewhere.

ARTHUR: Yes. She's got to be. I'm still waiting for her answer.

EUGENE: What? You mean she hasn't consented yet?

ARTHUR: She's got to. Everything else is ready now. She can't leave me in the lurch at a moment like this.

EUGENE: I don't mean to criticize you, Arthur, but haven't you rushed things a bit? I mean, shouldn't you have made sure of *her* before starting in on (*he points to the others with his pistol barrel*) these people?

ARTHUR: The time was ripe. I couldn't put it off.

EUGENE: Well, that's how it is with a *coup d'état*. Always some unforeseeable factor. Still, we can't back out now.

ARTHUR: Who could have dreamed of such a thing? I was so sure I had convinced her. (*He calls.*) Ala, Ala! (*Irritably.*) All because of some dumb cousin. Incredible! (*He calls.*) Ala, Ala.

EUGENE: Women have been the ruin of kingdoms and empires.

ALA (*enters*): Gosh, are you all still up?

ARTHUR (*reproachfully*): At last! I've been looking all over for you.

ALA: What's going on? Uncle with a gun? Is it real? Is Uncle real?

ARTHUR: That's none of your business. Where have you been?

ALA: Out for a walk. Anything wrong with that?

EUGENE: Yes! At this solemn hour, there is.

ARTHUR: Steady, Uncle. You're on duty, remember. (*To* ALA.) Well?

ALA: Well, what? It's a lovely night.

ARTHUR: I wasn't asking about the weather. Do you consent?

ALA: I think I need a little more time, Arthur.

ARTHUR: I need an answer immediately. You've had plenty of time.

Pause.

ALA: Yes.

EUGENE: Hurrah!

ARTHUR: Thank God! Now we can start!

He gives ALA *his arm and leads her to the sofa where* EUGENIA *is sitting.*

Grandmother, your blessing.

EUGENIA (*starts up from the sofa in a fright*): Oh, leave me alone. I haven't done anything to you.

ARTHUR: But Grandmother, everything's changed now. I'm going to marry Ala. Give us your blessing.

EUGENE (*to the others*): On your feet, everybody! Can't you see this is a solemn occasion?

ELEANOR: My goodness, is Arthur going to get married?

STOMIL: Is that any reason to make such a fuss?

EUGENIA: Get that boy out of here! He's going to torture me again.

ARTHUR (*menacingly*): Grandmother, your blessing.

STOMIL: A tasteless joke. It's gone on long enough now.

EUGENE (*triumphantly*): The jokes are over now. You've been having your jokes for fifty years. Stomil, button your pajamas immediately! Your son has just plighted his troth. The day of the wide-open fly is past. Bless them, Eugenia.

EUGENIA: What should I do, Eleanor?

ELEANOR: Give them your blessing if it means so much to them.

EUGENIA: Can't they do without it? It makes me feel so old.

EUGENE: A good old-fashioned engagement. Give them your blessing, or I'll shoot. I'm going to count to three. One . . .

STOMIL: This is incredible. If a man can't be comfortable in his own house . . . (*He tries to button his pajamas.*)

EUGENE: Two . . .

EUGENIA (*lays her hand on the heads of* ALA *and* ARTHUR): My blessing upon you, dear children . . . and now go to hell!

EUGENE (*moved*): Just like old times.

ARTHUR (*stands up and kisses Eugenia's hand*): We thank you, Grandmother.

EUGENE: Stomil has buttoned his fly! A whole new era has begun!

STOMIL: Eleanor! You're crying?

ELEANOR (*sobbing with emotion*): Forgive me . . . But Arthur's getting engaged . . . and after all he is our son . . . I know I'm being terribly old-fashioned, but it's so moving. Forgive me.

STOMIL: Oh, do what you want, all of you! (*He runs out of the room in a rage.*)

EDDIE: If you'll permit me, on this joyous occasion I would like to wish the young couple all the best for the days to come and especially . . .

Holds out his hand to ARTHUR.

ARTHUR (*not taking his hand*): You! To the kitchen!

He points dramatically to the kitchen door. EDDIE *saunters out.*

And stay there until you're called.

EUGENE: To the kitchen.

ELEANOR (*in tears*): When's the wedding?

ARTHUR: Tomorrow.

EUGENE: Hurray! We've won!

ACT THREE

Daylight. The same room, but with no trace now of the former disorder: a conventional middle-class living room of about fifty years ago. None of the previous confusion and blurred contours. The draperies which had been lying about, giving the impression of an unmade bed, are now hung in orderly fashion. The catafalque is still in its old place—the curtain in front of the alcove is drawn back— but it is covered with napkins and knicknacks, so that it looks like a buffet.

On stage ELEANOR, EUGENIA, STOMIL, and EUGENE. EUGENIA is sitting on the sofa in the middle of the room. She is wearing a bonnet and a dark gray or brown dress buttoned up to the neck and adorned with lace cuffs and ruching. She has a lorgnette which she frequently raises to her eyes. To her right sits ELEANOR with her hair done up in a chignon; she is wearing earrings and a striped violet or burgundy-colored dress gathered at the waist. Both sit bolt upright, immobile, their hands on their knees. Beside them stands STOMIL, his hair combed, pomaded and parted in the middle. His stiff collar forces him to stretch his head as though looking into the distance. He is wearing a brown suit that is obviously too tight for him, and white spats. He is resting one hand on a little round table on which stands a vase with flowers; the other is braced on his hip. One foot is balanced nonchalantly on the tip of his shoe. In front of the group near the proscenium, a large camera on a tripod, covered with black velvet. Behind the camera stands

EUGENE. *He is still wearing his black swallowtail coat but his khaki shorts have been replaced by long black trousers with pin stripes. A red carnation in his buttonhole. In front of him on the floor, his top hat, white gloves and a cane with a silver knob. He fusses with the camera while the others hold their pose.* EUGENIA *says "Ah . . . ah" several times and sneezes loudly.*

EUGENE: Don't move!
EUGENIA: I can't help it. It's the moth balls.
EUGENE: Hold it!

> STOMIL *removes his hand from his hip and scratches his chest.*

Stomil, your hand.
STOMIL: But I'm itching all over.
ELEANOR: Why should you be itching?
STOMIL: Moths.
ELEANOR: Moths! (*She jumps up and runs across the stage, chasing moths, occasionally clapping her hands.*)
EUGENE: At this rate we'll never get a picture. Sit down, Eleanor.
ELEANOR (*reproachfully*): The moths come from Mama.
EUGENIA: They do not. They come out of this old rag.
EUGENE: Let's not quarrel. They come from the attic.
EDDIE (*enters dressed as a valet, in a crimson vest with black stripes*): You called, Madame?
ELEANOR (*stops clapping her hands*): What? What is it now? Oh yes. My salts, Edward!
EDDIE: Salts, Madame?
ELEANOR: Those smelling salts . . . you know . . .
EDDIE: Certainly, Madame. (*He goes out.*)

STOMIL (*looking after him*): I must admit it's a relief to see that fellow put in his place.

EUGENE: You haven't seen anything yet. Everything's going splendidly. You won't regret a thing.

STOMIL (*tries to loosen his collar*): If only this collar weren't so damn tight!

EUGENE: That's the price you've got to pay for having Eddie wait on you. Everything has its price.

STOMIL: And my experiments? Will I have to give them up?

EUGENE: I couldn't say. Arthur hasn't announced his decision on that point yet.

STOMIL: Maybe he'll let me go on with them. He hasn't said anything?

EUGENE: There hasn't been time. He went out early this morning.

STOMIL: Perhaps you could put in a good word for me, Uncle?

EUGENE (*patronizingly*): I'll speak to him when the opportunity arises.

STOMIL: At least once a week. After all these years I can't just suddenly stop. You ought to realize that.

EUGENE: That will depend entirely on your conduct, Stomil.

STOMIL: But I'm on your side. What more do you want? I'm even putting up with this collar. (*He tries again to loosen it.*)

EUGENE: Well, I can't promise.

EDDIE *enters with a tray on which a bottle of vodka is very much in evidence.*

What is that?

EDDIE: The salts for Madame, sir.

EUGENE (*menacingly*): Eleanor, what is the meaning of this?

ELEANOR: I can't imagine. (*To* EDDIE.) I asked for my smelling salts.

EDDIE: Madame no longer drinks?

ELEANOR: Take it away immediately!

EUGENIA: Why? As long as he's brought it . . . I don't feel too well.

EDDIE: As you wish, Madame.

He goes out. On the way he takes a good swig from the bottle. Only EUGENIA, *looking after him longingly, notices.*

EUGENE: Don't let it happen again!

EUGENIA: God, am I bored!

EUGENE: Back to your places!

ELEANOR, STOMIL *and* EUGENIA *sit up and freeze as at the beginning of the act.* EUGENE *ducks under the velvet cloth, the ticking of the timer is heard.* EUGENE *reaches quickly for his stick, top hat and gloves, and takes a stance beside* EUGENIA. *The ticking stops. Relieved, they all relax.*

STOMIL: Can't I unbutton these buttons for just a second?

EUGENE: Certainly not! The wedding is at twelve!

STOMIL: I seem to have put on weight. The last time I wore these things was forty years ago.

EUGENE: You have only your experiments to blame for that. Experimental art pays so well these days.

STOMIL: That's not my fault, is it?

ELEANOR: When will that picture be ready? I think I blinked. I know I'm going to look simply awful.

EUGENE: Don't worry. The camera hasn't worked for years.

ELEANOR: What? Then why take the picture?

EUGENE: It's the principle of the thing. It's a tradition.

STOMIL: You begrudge me my innocent experiments but is an old-fashioned broken-down camera any better? You know what I think of your counterrevolution? It's a fiasco.

EUGENE: Watch your tongue.

STOMIL: I bow to superior force, but I can still say what I think.

ELEANOR (*to* EUGENIA): What do you say, Mother?

EUGENIA: I say we're in one hell of a mess and this is only the beginning.

EUGENE: It can't be helped. Our first job is to create the form. The content comes later.

STOMIL: You're making a colossal mistake, Eugene. Formalism will never free you from chaos. You'd be better off if you could just accept the spirit of the times.

EUGENE: That's enough out of you. Defeatism will not be tolerated!

STOMIL: All right, all right. I can still have an opinion, can't I?

EUGENE: Of course. As long as it agrees with ours.

ELEANOR: Listen!

Bells are heard in the distance.

STOMIL: Bells!

EUGENE: Wedding bells.

ALA *enters. She is wearing a wedding dress with a long veil.* STOMIL *kisses her hand.*

STOMIL: Ah, here comes our dear little bride!

ELEANOR: Oh, Ala, it's so becoming!

EUGENIA: My dear child!

ALA: Isn't Arthur back yet?

EUGENE: We're expecting him any minute. He had a few final formalities to attend to.

ALA: These damned formalities.

EUGENE: But the spirit of life can't run around naked. It must always be dressed with taste and care. You mean Arthur hasn't discussed that point with you yet?

ALA: For hours on end.

EUGENE: And rightly so. Someday you'll understand and be grateful to him.

ALA: Oh, stop making such an ass of yourself, Uncle.

ELEANOR: You mustn't talk like that, Ala dear. Today is your wedding day and no time for family quarrels. There'll be plenty of time for that later.

EUGENE: Don't worry. No offense. I quite understand.

ALA: So old and so stupid. I can understand it in Arthur. But you, Uncle . . .

ELEANOR: Ala!

STOMIL: He had it coming.

ELEANOR: Forgive her, Eugene. She's so excited she doesn't know what she's saying. After all, this is a big day in her life. I remember the day I was married to Stomil . . .

EUGENE: I can tell when I'm not wanted. But don't delude yourselves. You can laugh at me as much as you like but childish insults won't change a thing. Stomil, come with me. I have a proposition to make to you.

STOMIL: All right. Just don't try to brainwash me!

They go out.

ELEANOR: Mama, you might go for a stroll too.

EUGENIA: Anything you say. It's all the same to me. Either way I'll be bored to death. (*She goes out.*)

ELEANOR: There. Now we can talk. Tell me, what's happened?

ALA: Nothing.

ELEANOR: Something's bothering you. I can see that.

ALA: Nothing's bothering me. This veil doesn't fall quite right. Help me with it, will you, Mother?

ELEANOR: Of course. But you don't have to take that tone with me. With the others it's different. They're such fools.

ALA (*sits down at the mirror; the bells are still ringing*): Why do you all despise each other?

ELEANOR: I don't know. Maybe because we have no reason to respect each other.

ALA: Yourselves or each other?

ELEANOR: It comes to the same thing. Shall I fix your hair?

ALA: It's got to be done all over again.

She takes off her veil. ELEANOR *combs her hair.*

Are you happy, Mother?

ELEANOR: I beg your pardon?

ALA: I asked if you were happy. What's so funny about that?

ELEANOR: It's a very indiscreet question.

ALA: Why? Is it a disgrace to be happy?

ELEANOR: No, I wouldn't say that.

ALA: Then you're not very happy, are you? Because you're ashamed. People are always ashamed about not being happy. It's like having pimples or not doing your homework. It makes them feel guilty, almost criminal.

ELEANOR: "It is the right and duty of all to be happy, now that the new era has set us free." Stomil taught me that.

ALA: Oh. So that's why everybody's so ashamed nowadays. But how do *you* feel about it?

ELEANOR: I've always done as much as I could.

ALA: To make Stomil happy?

ELEANOR: No. Myself. That's the way he wanted it.

ALA: Then in a way it was for him?

ELEANOR: Of course it was for him. Oh, if you'd only known him when he was young . . .

ALA: It's not right yet on this side. Does he know?

ELEANOR: What?

ALA: Don't be like that. I'm not a baby. Your affair with Eddie.

ELEANOR: Of course he knows.

ALA: And what does he say?

ELEANOR: Nothing, unfortunately. He pretends not to notice.

ALA: That's bad.

EDDIE *comes in with a white tablecloth.*

EDDIE: May I set the table now?

ELEANOR: Sure, Eddie. (*She corrects herself.*) Yes, Edward, you may set the table.

EDDIE: Yes, Madame. (*He lays the cloth on the table and takes the camera out with him.*)

ALA: What do you see in him?

ELEANOR: Oh, he's just so simple . . . like life itself. He can be rough, of course, but that's the secret of his charm. A man without complexes—it's so refreshing. He just wants what he wants. Wonderful. And the way he sits —nothing unusual about it, but it's real, honest-to-goodness sitting. And when he eats, when he drinks! His stomach becomes a symphony of nature. I just love to watch him digest. It's so simple, so direct. It's like the elements. Have you ever noticed how divinely he hitches his trousers up? Stomil admires authenticity too.

ALA: I know. It doesn't fascinate me very much. I'm afraid.

ELEANOR: You're too young. You haven't had time to learn the value of genuine simplicity. You will. It takes experience.

ALA: I'll certainly try. Tell me, Mother, do you think it's a good idea for me to marry Arthur?

ELEANOR: Oh, Arthur is something else again. He has principles.

ALA: But Stomil has principles too. You said so yourself. All that stuff about the right and duty to be happy.

ELEANOR: Oh, those were only opinions. Stomil has always detested principles. Arthur, on the other hand, has cast-iron principles.

ALA: And that's all he has.

ELEANOR: Ala, how can you say a thing like that? Arthur's the first man in fifty years to have principles. Doesn't that appeal to you? It's so original! And it's so becoming to him!

ALA: You really think principles are enough for me?

ELEANOR: Well, I admit, they're rather old-fashioned. But so unusual these days . . .

ALA: I'll take Arthur with principles if I have to, Mother. But principles without Arthur—no.

ELEANOR: But didn't he propose to you? Isn't he going to marry you?

ALA: Not Arthur.

ELEANOR: Then who? What are you talking about?

ALA: His principles!

ELEANOR: Then why did you accept?

ALA: Because I still have hope.

ELEANOR: That, my dear, is fatal.

EDDIE *enters with a stack of plates.*

EDDIE: May I continue?

ALA: Clatter away, Eddie boy. (*Corrects herself.*) I mean, yes, Edward, clatter away. I mean, do continue, Edward.

ELEANOR: Tell me, Eddie, does it depress you? All these changes thought up by a bunch of fools?

EDDIE: Why should it depress me?

ELEANOR: Didn't I tell you? He's as free and natural as a butterfly. Oh, Eddie, you set the table so gracefully.

EDDIE: I'm not knocking myself out, that's for sure.

ALA: Eddie, come here.

EDDIE: At your service. What can I do for you, Miss?

Suddenly the bells fall silent.

ALA: Tell me, Eddie, have you got principles?

EDDIE: Principles? Sure.

ALA: What kind?

EDDIE: The best.

ALA: Tell me one. Please.

EDDIE: What's in it for me?

ALA: Well, can you or can't you?

EDDIE: If I have to, I guess. Just a sec. (*He puts the plates down on the floor and takes a little memo book from his pocket.*) I've got one written down here somewhere. (*He leafs through the book.*) Here it is! (*He reads.*) "I love you, and you're sound asleep."

ALA: That's all?

EDDIE: "You made your bed, now lie in it."

ALA: Oh, come on, Eddie. Read.

EDDIE: I did read. That's a principle.

ALA: Then read another!

EDDIE *giggles.*

What's so funny?

EDDIE: Well, there's one here . . .

ALA: Read it! . .

EDDIE: I can't, not in mixed company. It's too good.

ALA: And those are your principles?

EDDIE: Actually, no. I borrowed them from a friend who works for the movies.

ALA: You haven't got any of your own?

EDDIE (*proudly*): No.

ALA: Why not?

EDDIE: What do I need them for? I know my way around.

ELEANOR: Oh yes, Eddie. You certainly do.

> STOMIL *rushes in, pursued by* EUGENE *carrying a laced corset.* EDDIE *goes on setting the table.*

STOMIL: No, no! That's asking too much!

EUGENE: Take my word for it. You'll be glad once it's on.

ELEANOR: Now what's wrong?

STOMIL (*running from* EUGENE): He wants to strap me into that thing.

ELEANOR: What is it?

EUGENE: Great grandfather's corset. Indispensable. Pulls in the waist, guarantees a perfect figure for every occasion.

STOMIL: No, no, no. I'm wearing spats, I've got this collar on. What are you trying to do—kill me?

EUGENE: Now, Stomil, let's not do things by halves.

STOMIL: I've gone far enough. Let me live!

EUGENE: You're falling back into your old habits, Stomil. Come on. Stop making such a fuss. You admitted yourself you'd been putting on weight.

STOMIL: But I want to be fat! I want to live in harmony with nature!

EUGENE: You just don't want to be bothered. Come on. Don't fight it. It won't do any good.

STOMIL: Eleanor, save me!

ELEANOR: You don't think it might improve your looks?

STOMIL: My looks? What for? I'm a free fat artist.

He runs into his room. EUGENE *following. The door closes behind them.*

ELEANOR: These perpetual scenes. And you say you still have hope?

ALA: Yes.

ELEANOR: And if you're only deluding yourself?

ALA: What difference does it make?

ELEANOR (*tries to take her in her arms*): My poor Ala! . . .

ALA (*freeing herself*): You don't need to pity me. I can take care of myself.

ELEANOR: But what if things don't work out?

ALA: That's my secret.

ELEANOR: You won't tell even me?

ALA: It will be a surprise.

STOMIL'S VOICE: Help!

ELEANOR: That's Stomil.

ALA: Uncle Eugene is really overdoing it. Do you think he has any influence on Arthur?

STOMIL'S VOICE: Let me go!

ELEANOR: I doubt it. It's probably the other way around.

ALA: Too bad. I thought it was all Uncle's fault.

STOMIL'S VOICE: Get out of here!

ELEANOR: I'd better go see what they're up to. I have a feeling something awful is going to happen.

ALA: So do I.

STOMIL'S VOICE: Murderer! Let me go!

ELEANOR: Good God, how will it all end?

STOMIL'S VOICE: No, no! I'll burst! I'll explode! Help!

ELEANOR: Eugene's going too far. But you, Ala, do be careful.

ALA: Careful?

ELEANOR: Don't go too far—like Uncle Eugene. (*She goes into Stomil's room.*)

ALA: Eddie, my veil!

> EDDIE *hands her the veil and stands behind her. From Stomil's room screaming and the sound of a struggle are heard.* ARTHUR *enters.* ALA *and* EDDIE *don't notice him. Arthur's coat is open. He looks gray. His listless, unnatural movements show that he is having great difficulty keeping himself going. He carefully removes his coat and throws it down somewhere. Sits down in an armchair and sprawls out his legs.*

STOMIL'S VOICE: Damn you!

ARTHUR (*in a low, dull voice*): What's going on?

> ALA *turns around.* EDDIE *dutifully picks up* ARTHUR'S *coat and goes out.*

ALA (*as though merely making an observation*): You're late.

> ARTHUR *stands up and opens Stomil's door.*

ARTHUR: Let him go.

> STOMIL, EUGENE *and then* ELEANOR *come out of the room.*

EUGENE: Why? It would have given him that final polish.

ARTHUR: I said let him go.

STOMIL: Thank you, Arthur. I'm glad to see you're not completely devoid of human feeling.

EUGENE: I protest!

> ARTHUR *grabs him by the tie and pushes him back.*

ELEANOR: Arthur, what's happened? He's as pale as a ghost!

ARTHUR: You whited skeleton!

EUGENE: Arthur, it's me, it's your Uncle Eugene! Don't you know me? You and I together . . . the new life . . . saving the world. Don't you remember? You're choking me. You and I . . . together . . . Don't . .

ARTHUR (*pushing him back step by step*): You stuffed zero, you synthetic blob . . . you worm-eaten false bottom!

ELEANOR: Do something! He's choking him!

ARTHUR: You fake . . .

Mendelssohn's "Wedding March" resounds, loud and triumphant. ARTHUR *lets* EUGENE *go, picks up a carafe from the table and hurls it off stage where it lands with a loud crash. The march breaks off in the middle of a measure.* ARTHUR *sinks into an armchair.*

EDDIE (*enters*): Do you wish me to change the record?

ELEANOR: Who told you to put that on?

EDDIE: Mr. Eugene. His orders were to put it on as soon as Mr. Arthur entered the room.

EUGENE (*gasping for air*): My orders. Yes, that's right.

ELEANOR: We won't need any music right now.

EDDIE: As you wish, Madame. (*He goes out.*)

ARTHUR: It's a fraud . . . The whole thing . . . a fraud! (*He collapses.*)

STOMIL (*leans over him*): He's dead drunk.

EUGENE: That's a slander, an infamous slander. This young man knows his duty. He's the soul of moderation.

ELEANOR: I can't believe it either. Arthur never drinks.

STOMIL: Take it from me. I'm an expert.

ELEANOR: But why today of all days?

STOMIL: His last hours as a free man.

ALA *pours water into a glass and feeds it to* ARTHUR.

EUGENE: There must be some misunderstanding. It would be unwise to draw premature conclusions. The truth will soon be known.

STOMIL: Yes. If we wait just a minute, he'll explain. He was just getting started.

ELEANOR: Shh . . . he's coming to.

ARTHUR (*raises his head and points to* STOMIL): What on earth is that?

ELEANOR: He doesn't know his own father. Ohhh! (*She bursts into tears.*)

ARTHUR: Quiet, you females! It's not my parents I'm asking about. What's the meaning of this masquerade?

STOMIL (*looking at his legs*): These . . . these are spats.

ARTHUR: Oh . . . yes, of course. They're spats. (*He sinks into thought.*)

EUGENE: Arthur's a little tired. Conditions will return to normal in a moment. Take your places. Attention! There will be no change in the program. (*To* ARTHUR *in a very friendly tone:*) Ha ha, well, Arthur, my boy, you were just joking, weren't you? Putting us to the test, you little devil! Don't worry. We won't abandon our positions. Here we are, all buttoned up from top to toe, once and for all. Stomil was even going to put on a corset. Cheer up, my boy. A little rest, and then . . . on with the wedding!

STOMIL: Same old song and dance! Can't you see, you ghost of the past, that he's stewed to the gills? His father's son all right.

EUGENE: That's a lie! Quiet! Come on, Arthur. It's time for action now. Everything's ready. Just one last step.

ARTHUR (*goes down on his knees to* STOMIL): Father, forgive me.

STOMIL: What's this? Some new trick?

ARTHUR (*dragging himself after* STOMIL *on his knees*): I was insane! There's no going back, no present, no future. There's nothing.

STOMIL (*evading him*): What is he now? A nihilist?

ALA (*tearing off her veil*): What about me? Am I nothing?

ARTHUR (*changing direction and dragging himself after her*): You too . . . forgive me!

ALA: You're a coward, that's all you are. A child and a coward and impotent!

ARTHUR: No, please don't say that. I'm not afraid, but I can't believe anymore. I'll do anything. I'll lay down my life . . . but there's no turning back to the old forms. They can't create a reality for us. I was wrong.

ALA: What are you talking about?

ARTHUR: About creating a world.

ALA: And me? Isn't anybody going to say anything about me?

EUGENE: This is treason!

ARTHUR (*changing direction again and heading for* EUGENE): You must forgive me too. I raised your hopes and I've let you down. But believe me, it's impossible . . .

EUGENE: I refuse to listen to this kind of talk. Pull yourself together. Stand up and get married. Raise a family, brush your teeth, eat with a knife and fork, make the world sit up straight. You'll see, we'll do it yet. You're not going to throw away our last chance, are you, Arthur?

ARTHUR: There never was a chance. We were wrong. It's hopeless.

EUGENE: Stomil's right. You're drunk. You don't know what you're saying.

ARTHUR: Yes, drunk. When I was sober I let myself be deceived, so I got drunk to dispel my illusions. You'd better have a drink too, Uncle

EUGENE: Me? Certainly not. . . . Well, perhaps just a little one. (*He pours himself a shot of vodka and downs it at one gulp.*)

ARTHUR: I had cold sober reasons for getting drunk. I drank myself sane again.

STOMIL: Nonsense. You got drunk out of despair.

ARTHUR: Yes, despair too. Despair that form can never save the world.

EUGENE: Then what can?

ARTHUR (*stands up, solemnly*): An idea!

EUGENE: What idea?

ARTHUR: If I only knew. Conventions always spring from an idea. Father was right. I'm a contemptible formalist.

STOMIL: Don't take it so hard, son. You know I've always been indulgent. Frankly, though, I've suffered plenty from your ideas. Thank God, that's all over now. (*Starts taking off his morning coat.*) Where are my pajamas?

ARTHUR (*rushes over to him and prevents him from taking off his coat*): Stop! A reversion to pajamas is equally impossible.

STOMIL: Why? Are you still trying to save us? I thought you'd got over that.

ARTHUR (*aggressively, going from one extreme to the other as drunks do; triumphantly*): Did you think I was going to cave in completely just like that?

STOMIL: Just a minute ago you were acting like a human being. Don't tell me you want to be an apostle again.

ARTHUR (*releasing* STOMIL, *with emphasis*): My sin was reason . . . and abstraction, the lewd daughter of reason. Now I have drowned my reason in alcohol. I didn't get drunk the usual way. Though my aim was mystical, I drank most rationally. The fire water cleansed me. You've got to forgive me because I stand before you purified. I clothed you in vestments and tore them off again because they proved to be shrouds. But I will not abandon you, naked, to the gales of history; I'd rather have you curse me. Eddie!

EDDIE *enters*.

Shut the door.

ELEANOR: Yes, Eddie, shut the door, there's a draft.

ARTHUR: Don't let anybody leave.

EDDIE: Okay, boss.

STOMIL: This is a violation of civil rights!

ARTHUR: You want freedom? There is no freedom from life, and life is synthesis. You'd analyze yourselves to death. Luckily, however, you have me.

EUGENE: Arthur, you know I don't agree with Stomil. But aren't you going a little too far? I feel it's my duty to warn you. In spite of everything, I stand by the freedom of the individual.

ARTHUR: Good. Now what we need is to find an idea.

STOMIL (*simultaneously with* EUGENE *and* ELEANOR): Is this any way to treat your father?

EUGENE: I wash my hands of the whole business.

ELEANOR: Arthur, lie down for a while. I'll make you a nice cold compress.

ARTHUR: Until we come up with an idea, nobody leaves this room. Eddie. Guard the door!

EDDIE: Yes, sir.

Pause.

ELEANOR: Find him an idea, somebody, so he'll leave us alone. If I don't go to the kitchen, the cake will be burned to a crisp.

EUGENE: Better humor him.

ARTHUR: What do you suggest, Uncle?

EUGENE: Search me . . . God, maybe?

ARTHUR: That's been done. Lost His appeal.

EUGENE: True. Even in my time there wasn't much you could do with God. I grew up in an age of enlightenment and exact science. I only mentioned Him for the sake of form.

ARTHUR: Forget about form. What we're after now is a living idea.

EUGENE: How about sports? I used to ride horseback.

ARTHUR: Everybody goes in for sports nowadays. A lot of good it does them.

EUGENE: Sorry. Maybe Stomil has an idea.

STOMIL: Experiment. There's an idea.

ARTHUR: Please, this is serious.

STOMIL: Well, I'm serious too. Blazing trails, opening new frontiers! Man is always looking for new worlds to conquer and conquest comes from experiment. From trial and error. But always with an aim in view: the new life, radically new!

ARTHUR: A new life! I don't even know what to do with the old one.

STOMIL: Well, everything is still in the experimental stage, that's why.

EUGENE: Eleanor, have you got an idea?

ARTHUR: There's no sense asking a woman.

ELEANOR: I had an idea, but I've forgotten. I'm supposed to

look after everything. Why don't you ask Eddie? He's got a good head on his shoulders, and when he does say something, you can depend on it.

STOMIL: That's right. Eddie is the collective mind.

ARTHUR: Well, what do you say then, Eddie?

EDDIE: Well, if anybody were to ask me, I'd say progress, sir.

ARTHUR: Meaning what?

EDDIE: Well, just that, sir: progress.

ARTHUR: But what kind of progress?

EDDIE: The progressive kind, the kind that goes right ahead.

ARTHUR: You mean forward?

EDDIE: Right. With the front moving forward.

ARTHUR: And the back?

EDDIE: The back moving forward too. Right out there in front.

ARTHUR: Then the front is in back?

EDDIE: Depends on how you look at it. If you look from back to front, the front is in front, though somehow or other it's also in back.

ARTHUR: That doesn't sound very clear to me.

EDDIE: No. But it's progressive.

EUGENIA *enters, leaning on a cane.*

EUGENIA (*timidly*): There's something I must tell you . . .

ELEANOR: Not now, Mother. Can't you see the men are discussing politics?

EUGENIA: Just two words . . .

ARTHUR: No, I don't like it. I need an idea that naturally, inevitably, leads to form. Your kind of progress leads nowhere.

EUGENIA: Please listen to me, my darlings. I won't take much of your time.

STOMIL: What is it now?

ELEANOR: I don't know. Something's wrong with Mama.

STOMIL: Later. We're busy now. (*To* ARTHUR.) I still say we should get back to experiments. Then the idea will come by itself.

EUGENIA *takes the knicknacks and napkins off the catafalque.*

ELEANOR: What are you doing, Mama?

EUGENIA (*matter-of-factly*): I'm dying.

ELEANOR: Mother! That's not very funny, you know.

Silently EUGENIA *tidies up the catafalque. She wipes away the dust with her sleeve.*

Mother says she's dying.

EUGENE: What? Dying? Can't she see we're busy?

ELEANOR: Did you hear that, Mama?

EUGENIA: Help me.

Involuntarily ELEANOR *gives her her arm.* EUGENIA *climbs up on the catafalque.*

ELEANOR: But don't be silly, Mama. There's going to be a wedding today. You wouldn't want to spoil everything by dying, would you?

STOMIL: Dying? What's all this about death? I never thought about that . . .

ARTHUR (*to himself*): Death? Excellent idea! . . .

EUGENE: This is ridiculous, Eugenia. Pull yourself together. This is no way to behave.

ALA: It wouldn't be normal, Grandmother.

EUGENIA: I don't understand you people. You're all so intelligent, but if somebody wants to do something as simple as dying, you don't know what to make of it. Really, you are very strange people. (*She lies down on her back and folds her hands over her breast.*)

ELEANOR: Look at her. Do something . . . Maybe she's really . . .

EUGENE: Eugenia, this is carrying eccentricity too far. This sort of thing isn't done in our family.

STOMIL: It's sheer hypocrisy.

EUGENIA: You'll find the key to my room on the table. I won't need it anymore. I'll be able to come and go as I please. The cards are in the drawer. All marked . . .

ARTHUR: Death . . . the supreme form!

STOMIL: Not exactly viable, though, is it?

ARTHUR: Why not? When it's somebody else's death.

He seems to have had a revelation, beats his forehead.

Grandma, you're brilliant!

ELEANOR: You ought to be ashamed of yourself! You all ought to be ashamed of yourselves.

EUGENE: Eugenia, lie properly at least. You're all hunched up. Elbows at your sides. Or get up this minute. Dying is no way to behave in society. Death is irrational.

STOMIL: Death is final and therefore no good as an experiment. An experiment has to be repeatable. Of course, if you're only rehearsing, that's something else again. But even so, there's not much point in it.

ALA: Stop! Can't you see what's happening?

EUGENIA: Come closer, my children.

All except EDDIE *go over to the catafalque.*

Eddie, you too!

EDDIE *joins the others.*

Who are you?

EUGENE: We're . . . it's just us.

EUGENIA *starts giggling, first softly, then loudly.*

Now she's insulting us. Did I say something funny?

STOMIL: I'm not feeling so well myself. Must be a headache. (*He steps aside, feels his pulse, takes a mirror out of his pocket, and looks at his tongue.*)

ARTHUR: Thank you, Grandmother, I'll make use of your idea.

STOMIL (*putting the mirror away*): Nothing serious, I guess. Must be these tight clothes.

EUGENIA *dies.*

ELEANOR: Try again, Mama.

ARTHUR: She's dead. Strange. She was always so frivolous.

ALA: I can't stand it!

EUGENE: I don't understand.

STOMIL: I don't want to have anything to do with this.

ELEANOR: I never dreamed . . . Stomil, why didn't you warn me?

STOMIL: Of course, it's all my fault. Frankly I don't see that this changes anything at all. My collar's as tight as ever.

ARTHUR (*drawing the curtain in front of the catafalque*): Eddie, come here.

EDDIE *comes over and stands at attention.* ARTHUR *feels his muscle.*

You pack a good punch, don't you?

EDDIE: Not bad, sir.

ARTHUR: And if necessary, you could . . ? (*He runs his finger across his throat.*)

EDDIE (*phlegmatically after a pause*): You ask me a question, Mr. Arthur? I'm not sure I heard you right.

Pause. ARTHUR *laughs, unsure of himself, as though waiting to see.* EDDIE *laughs with a similar "ha ha."*

ARTHUR *laughs once again more loudly and with more assurance. Whereupon* EDDIE *utters a resounding laugh.* ARTHUR *slaps him on the shoulder.*

ARTHUR: Eddie, I like you. I've always liked you.

EDDIE: And I've always thought we'd understand each other someday.

ARTHUR: Then you do understand?

EDDIE: Eddie understands all right.

STOMIL: This business has rather upset me. I'm going to lie down for a while.

ARTHUR: Stay right where you are, Father.

STOMIL: Oh stop ordering me around, you little punk. I'm tired. (*He starts for his room.*)

ARTHUR: Eddie!

EDDIE *bars Stomil's way.*

STOMIL: Who do you think you are? (*Furiously pointing at* EDDIE, *to* ELEANOR:) And you've been having an affair with this flunky?

ELEANOR: For God's sake, not now. Not with Mama lying there.

EDDIE *pushes* STOMIL *into an armchair.*

ARTHUR: Just a bit more patience, please. It's all quite clear to me now. I shall show you the way to a better future.

EUGENE (*sitting down with resignation*): I just don't seem to care anymore . . . I must be getting old. We're just not as young as we used to be, are we, Stomil?

STOMIL: Speak for yourself. You're almost as old as Eugenia was, you old hypocrite. I feel fine. By and large. (*Pleading.*) Eleanor, where are you?

ELEANOR: Here, Stomil, right beside you.

STOMIL: Come here.

ELEANOR (*resting her hand on his forehead*): How do you feel?

STOMIL: I don't know what's wrong, but not well at all.

ARTHUR: Uncertainty and indecision are behind us now. Now the road lies before us, straight and clear. From now on there will be only one law and one herd.

STOMIL: What's he jabbering about now? . . . Oh, my head!

EUGENE: Something about a new legal code for livestock.

ARTHUR: Don't you see the logical conclusion? Ah, creatures of flesh, caught up in your glandular secretions and terrified at the thought of your death, *are you incapable of all understanding?* But I understand! Unthinking cattle, behold your redeemer! I have risen above this world, and I will draw you all up after me, because I alone have a brain freed from the snares of the bowels.

EUGENE: Instead of insulting us, my dear great-nephew, kindly express yourself more clearly.

ARTHUR: Won't you ever understand, you whose lives rot away like mushrooms? You're like blind puppies that would walk in circles forever if they had no master to lead them. Without form or ideas, you would crumble to chaos and be consumed by the void if I weren't on hand to save you. Do you know what I'm going to do with you? I'm going to create a system in which rebellion will be combined with order, nonbeing with being. I will transcend all contradictions.

EUGENE: It would perhaps be better if you'd just leave the room. You've disappointed me. It's all over between us. (*To himself.*) I'll probably return to writing my memoirs.

ARTHUR: Let me just ask you this: if nothing exists and if even rebellion is impossible, then what *can* be raised up out of this nothingness and made to exist?

EUGENE (*takes out a watch with a little chain*): It's late. We could all do with a bite to eat.

ARTHUR: Isn't anybody going to answer me?

STOMIL: Eleanor, what are we having for lunch today? I'd like something light. My stomach's a bit queasy. It's high time we took better care of it.

ELEANOR: You're right, Stomil. From now on we'll look after you. A little nap after lunch, a little stroll after napping. The morning will be for experiments.

STOMIL: And everything cooked in butter, or maybe cut out fats entirely.

ELEANOR: Yes. We'll sleep better that way too.

ARTHUR: What? Silence? All right, I'll tell you. (*He puts his chair on the set table, climbs reeling on the table and sits down in the chair.*)

ELEANOR: Careful of the dishes, Arthur.

ARTHUR: The only possible answer is power.

EUGENE: Power? What power? We're your family, remember?

STOMIL: He's raving. Don't pay any attention to him.

ARTHUR: Power alone can exist in a vacuum. Now I am up here above you, and you are beneath me.

EUGENE: Brilliant, isn't he?

ELEANOR: Arthur, come down. You're getting the table-cloth all dirty.

ARTHUR: You grovel beneath me in dust and ashes.

EUGENE: How long are we going to put up with this?

STOMIL: Let him talk. We'll take care of him after lunch. It's beyond me where he gets these tendencies. Must be his upbringing.

ARTHUR: Everything depends on being strong and decisive. I am strong. Look at me then. I am the answer to your dreams. Uncle Eugene, there will be order. Father, you have always rebelled, but your rebellion consumed itself in chaos. Now look at me. Power, too, is rebellion. A revolution in form and order, the revolt of the top against the bottom, the high against the low. The mountain needs the plain and the plain needs the mountain, otherwise each would cease to be what it is. Power resolves the paradox of opposites. Neither synthesis nor analysis, I am the act, the will and the way. I am power. I am above, within and beside all things. Give thanks to me for fulfilling the dreams of your youth. This is my gift to you. Yet I have a gift for myself as well: the form I have always longed for. For I can now create and destroy not just one but a thousand possible forms. I can incarnate and disincarnate myself. I have here within me—everything. (*He beats his breast.*)

EUGENE: Poor boy. Sad to see a thing like this happen.

STOMIL: Oh don't take it so seriously. Adolescent foolishness. Words, words, words. What power has he got over us?

EUGENE: Right! What does all his talk amount to anyway? We're united by blood, not by abstractions. He can't do a thing to us.

ARTHUR: It's very simple. I can kill you.

STOMIL (*rises from his chair and falls back again*): I absolutely forbid you . . . There are limits.

ARTHUR: Limits can be transcended. *You* taught me that. Power over life and death. What greater power can there be? A simple but profoundly important discovery!

EUGENE: Nonsense! I'll live as long as I please. That is, I mean, as long as it pleases. . . . I don't know whom, do you, Stomil?

STOMIL: Well . . . Nature?

EUGENE: Exactly. Nature or fate.

ARTHUR: No. *Me!*

EUGENE (*jumping up*): Don't make me laugh!

ARTHUR: But suppose I become your fate, Uncle?

EUGENE: Eleanor, Stomil, what does this mean? I won't stand for it. He's your son, after all.

ELEANOR: Look what you've done, Arthur. You've frightened your uncle. He's white as a sheet. Don't get up, Stomil. I'll get you a pillow.

ARTHUR: Did you really think I'd start something I couldn't finish? Each one of you has a death shut inside you like a nightingale locked in a cage. All I have to do is let it out. Well, do you still think I'm a utopian, a babbler, a dreamer?

EUGENE: Ha ha! There's no getting around it, Arthur— you've got a head on your shoulders. You've thought this whole thing out very nicely. Nothing like a good university education, I always say. Hopeless to argue with you; you'll always win. But while we talk, time is flying and though there's nothing I enjoy more than a philosophico-scientific discussion, especially with the younger generation, we've talked long enough. Our horizons have been expanded, but now it's time for something concrete. Enough theory. Let's have something to eat. What do you say, Eleanor?

ELEANOR: I wanted to suggest that some time ago, but I couldn't get a word in edgewise. Enough now, Arthur, come down. Or at least take your shoes off.

ARTHUR: You're right, Uncle, it's time for something concrete. Eddie, my dark angel, are you ready?

EDDIE: Ready, chief.

ARTHUR: Then grab him.

EUGENE (*trying to escape*): What are you going to do?

ARTHUR: First we're going to rub out Uncle Eugene.

ELEANOR: Rub out? Where on earth did you pick that up?

STOMIL: And now of all times, with my blood pressure sky-rocketing!

EUGENE (*still trying to reach the door*): Why me?

EDDIE *bars the way.*

ARTHUR: So I'm all just theory, am I? Eddie, show him he's mistaken. You trash! What do you take me for?

EDDIE *tries to catch* EUGENE.

EUGENE: This isn't a system. It's mob rule.

ARTHUR: Do your duty, Eddie.

EUGENE (*running from* EDDIE, *who follows him with sure, catlike movements*): What does this ape want of me? Keep your hands off me!

ARTHUR: He's not an ape. He's the right arm of my spirit, my word made flesh.

STOMIL (*tearing his collar open*): Eleanor, I feel awful. Eleanor!

ELEANOR: Look, your father's fainted.

EUGENE (*still running away*): Madman! Murderer!

ARTHUR (*stands up and stretches out his arm*): No! A man who has seen the one possibility and doesn't shrink from it. I am as pure as nature. I am free. Free!

ALA: Arthur! . . .

ARTHUR: Wait. First we've got to save the world.

ALA: I've been unfaithful to you. With Eddie.

EDDIE *and* EUGENE *suddenly stop still and look at* ARTHUR *and* ALA. ELEANOR *is busy slapping Stomil's checks, trying to rouse him from his faint.*

ARTHUR (*slowly lowering his arms, after a moment of silence*): What?

ALA: I didn't think you'd mind. After all, you only wanted to marry me out of principle.

ARTHUR (*sits down, dazed*): When?

ALA: This morning.

ARTHUR (*to himself*): I see . . .

ALA: I didn't think you'd care. I thought . . . Look, I'm ready for the wedding. (*She puts on her veil.*) How do I look?

ARTHUR (*gropes his way clumsily off the table*): Wait a second, wait . . . You? You did that to me?

ALA (*with affected nonchalance*): I forgot to tell you. You were so busy . . . We can go now. Should I wear my gloves? They're a bit tight. You like the way I've done my hair?

ARTHUR (*bellowing*): You did that to *me?*

ALA (*affecting surprise*): You still going on about that? I didn't think you'd even be interested. Let's change the subject, shall we?

ARTHUR (*in a state of collapse, gropes his way around the table; he seems to have lost control over his movements; in a plaintive monotone*): How could you . . . how could you?

ALA: But you said you only needed me to help you with your plan. Don't you remember? I didn't misunderstand you, did I? Yesterday, when we were talking and you said such clever things, I was impressed. Really. Eddie could never have spoken like that.

ARTHUR (*bellowing*): Eddie!

ALA: Eddie's something else again.

ARTHUR (*plaintively*): Why did you do that to me?

ALA: What's got into you, darling? I've told you, I didn't think you'd care. Frankly, I'm surprised at you, making such a fuss over nothing. Now I'm sorry I even told you.

ARTHUR: But why?

ALA: Oh, my stubborn darling! I had my reasons.

ARTHUR (*shouting*): What reasons?

ALA: Let's forget about it. You're just getting yourself all worked up.

ARTHUR: Tell me!

ALA: I only wanted to . . .

ARTHUR: Go on. Your reasons . . .

ALA (*frightened*): Oh, the stupidest, silliest little reasons . . .

ARTHUR: Go on!

ALA: I won't tell you. You always get mad.

ARTHUR: Oh God!

ALA: If you want, we'll never say another word about the whole thing. Is it all my fault?

ARTHUR (*goes up to* STOMIL *and* ELEANOR): Why are you all against me? What have I done to you? Mother, did you hear that?

ELEANOR: Ala, I warned you.

ARTHUR (*clinging to* ELEANOR): Mama, tell her she mustn't do such things. Do something, help me, I can't live like this. Tell her . . . How can she treat me like this . . . (*He bursts into tears.*)

ELEANOR (*tearing herself away from him*): Get away from me, you silly child.

ARTHUR (*repulsed, staggers to the center of the stage; tearfully*): I wanted to save you. I was so close . . . And now you've ruined it all. Ah, the world is evil, evil, evil.

ALA: Come to me, Arthur! (*She goes toward him.*) Oh, my poor boy, I feel so sorry for you.

ARTHUR (*shoving her away*): You! Sorry for me? You dare to pity me? I don't need anyone's pity. You don't know me yet . . . but you're going to now. All right.

You've rejected my idea. You've trampled me under-
foot. (*To* ALA.) And you besmirched the noblest idea
in all history, you goose! Oh! What blindness! You
can't even begin to imagine who it is you've lost. And
who did you do it with? With this half-witted punk,
this garbage dumped out by our times. I'll go away,
but I won't leave you behind in this world. You don't
know what you're living for anyway. Where is he, your
darling lover? Where's that rotten beer belly anyway?
I'll fix that early bird's guts! (*He runs desperately
around the room, looking blindly for something on the
tables and on the sofa.*) The revolver! Where can it
be? It's impossible to find anything with all this
damned order! Mama, have you seen the revolver?

EDDIE *creeps up from behind, takes the revolver from
his breast pocket, and, taking a wide swing, hits*
ARTHUR *in the back of the neck with the butt.* ARTHUR
sinks to his knees. EDDIE *tosses the revolver aside,
pushes Arthur's head deftly forward so that it hangs
down, clasps his hands and, raising himself on his
tiptoes, swings his hands down on Arthur's head like
an ax.* ARTHUR *falls over, hitting the floor with his forehead. This scene must look very realistic.*

ALA (*kneels beside* ARTHUR): Arthur!
ELEANOR (*kneels on the other side of* ARTHUR): Arthur! My
son!
EDDIE (*steps aside, looks at his hands, with surprise*): Hm,
that was hard.
ARTHUR (*slowly and softly, as though amazed*): Strange . . .
everything's disappeared . . .
ALA: But I didn't want . . . It's not true!
EDDIE: Ha ha ha!

ARTHUR (*still with his face on the floor, very softly*): I loved you, Ala.

ALA: Why didn't you tell me before?

EDDIE: "I love you and you're sound asleep."

ELEANOR (*runs to* STOMIL *and shakes him*): Wake up. Your son is dying!

STOMIL (*opening his eyes*): Can't you people spare me anything?

He stands up with difficulty and leaning on ELEANOR *approaches* ARTHUR. ELEANOR, STOMIL *and* EUGENE *stand over him.* ALA *kneels.* EDDIE *to one side makes himself comfortable in an armchair.*

ARTHUR (*stretching out on the floor*): I wanted . . . I wanted . . . (*pause*).

ALA (*stands up; matter-of-factly*): He's dead.

EUGENE: Perhaps he's better off. He nearly murdered his uncle.

STOMIL: Forgive him. He wasn't happy.

EUGENE (*magnanimously*): Oh, I don't bear him any grudge. He can't hurt me now.

STOMIL: He tried to overcome indifference and mediocrity. He lived for reason, but lived too passionately. He died because his thought had betrayed his feelings.

EDDIE: He meant well, but he was too highstrung. His kind never gets old.

All turn toward EDDIE.

STOMIL: Hold your tongue, you scoundrel, and get out of my house. You ought to be glad to get off so easy.

EDDIE: Why should I leave? I'll say it again: he meant well. I'm staying.

STOMIL: Why?

EDDIE: It's my turn now. Now you're all going to listen to me.

STOMIL: We listen? To you?

EDDIE: Sure, why not? You've seen that I pack a wicked punch. Nothing to worry about so long as you keep quiet and do what I say. You'll see. You won't have to worry. I'm a regular guy. I like a joke, like a good time. But get this: There's got to be order.

EUGENE: We're in for it now.

EDDIE: You know, you talk too much. Take my shoes off for me, will you?

EUGENE: I submit to brute force. But I'll despise him in my heart.

EDDIE: Go ahead and despise me, but now take my shoes off, and quick.

EUGENE *kneels in front of him and takes his shoes off.*

STOMIL: I've always thought we were slaves of abstractions, but that someday humanity would take its revenge. Now I see that it's only Eddie.

ELEANOR: Maybe it won't be so bad. He certainly won't mind if you diet.

EUGENE (*holding the shoes*): Should I shine them, sir?

EDDIE: No, you can have 'em. I'm changing anyway. (*He stands up, takes off Arthur's jacket, puts it on and looks at himself in the mirror.*) A little tight, but not bad!

STOMIL: Come, Eleanor. We're only a poor old couple now.

EDDIE: Don't go too far, and be ready to come running when I call.

ELEANOR: Are you coming with us, Ala?

ALA: I'm coming. He loved me, nobody can take that away from me.

STOMIL (*to himself*): We may as well assume it was love.
ALA: Did you say something, Father?
STOMIL: Me? No.

> ELEANOR *and* STOMIL *go out, holding hands.* ALA
> *follows.* EDDIE *takes various poses and expressions be-*
> *fore the mirror, thrusts out his lower jaw, puts one*
> *hand on his hip.* EUGENE *runs up and down with*
> *Eddie's shoes, finally stops beside* ARTHUR.

EUGENE: I've got the feeling, Arthur, my boy, that nobody
needs you anymore.

> *He stands there meditating.* EDDIE *goes out and comes*
> *back with a tape recorder. Puts it on the table and plugs*
> *it in. Immediately the tango "La Cumparsita" re-*
> *sounds very loud and clear. It must be this tango and*
> *no other.*

EDDIE: Well, Uncle Eugene, would you like to dance?
EUGENE: Me? With you . . . Oh, all right, why not?

> EUGENE *puts down the shoes beside* ARTHUR. EDDIE
> *puts his arm around him. They take the proper posi-*
> *tion, wait out one measure and start dancing.* EDDIE
> *leads. They dance.* EUGENE *still has the red carnation*
> *in his buttonhole.* EDDIE *in Arthur's jacket that is too*
> *tight for him, his powerful arms protruding from the*
> *sleeves that are too short. He has taken* EUGENE *by the*
> *waist. They dance all the figures of the tango. The*
> *curtain falls. "La Cumparsita" is still heard. As the*
> *light goes on in the theater, the tune issues from nu-*
> *merous loudspeakers throughout the house.*

· **END**